KENNY OF THE CELTIC

Stephen Murray

Foreword by Hugh MacDonald

Published by CQN Books, Scotland.

Copyright Stephen Murray. All rights reserved.

First published in the United Kingdom in 2016 by CQN Books
ISBN 978-0-9934360-8-6

A catalogue for this book is available from the British Library
and the Irish Library in Dublin.

Cover & page design and typesetting
by Stephen Cameron for CQN Books.

Publisher, David Faulds for CQN Books.

Printed by APS, Airdrie, North Lanarkshire

A special thank you to everyone in the
Celtic Quick News community and the wider Celtic family.

CQN has published books on Lisbon Lions Willie Wallace,
Tommy Gemmell, Charlie Gallagher and John Hughes.
Hoops, Stars & Stripes: The Andy Lynch Story
by Paul John Dykes alongside Caesar & The Assassin
and The Winds of Change by Alex Gordon.

For the latest Celtic news and best Celtic conversation
visit www.celticquicknews.co.uk
and to shop online at www.cqnbookstore.com

ABOUT THE AUTHOR

Stephen Murray is a lifelong Celtic fan. Kenny of the Celtic is his second book. His previous publication, Ten Men Won The League, is available at Amazon. Stephen also writes for The Celtic Underground website, and is a regular contributor to the Celtic match day programme.

DEDICATION

To my late father, Dominick Murray,
for passing on a great love of Celtic.

And to all those who ever stood on the
old Celtic end terracing, cheering on the team.

KENNY OF THE CELTIC

Celtic supporters have an endearing habit of referring to some of their greatest heroes by their full names - James Edward McGrory, Charles Patrick Tully, James Connolly Johnstone and Daniel Fergus McGrain. But perhaps the best known of all Celts with a triad of names is a certain Kenneth Mathieson Dalglish.

Kenny Dalglish represented Celtic with huge distinction from 1968 to 1977, and is regarded as one of the club's greatest players, in the company of Patsy Gallagher, Jimmy McGrory, Jimmy Johnstone and Henrik Larsson.

This book tells of how Kenny progressed from modest beginnings, through the ranks at Parkhead, becoming possibly the finest footballer Scotland has ever produced, before departing for Liverpool in 1977. In his biography of Jock Stein, respected football historian Bob Crampsey rated Dalglish as the best player in British football between 1970 and 1985.

Kenny started his career at Celtic as a member of the *'Quality Street Gang'*, the name affectionately given to Scottish football's greatest ever reserve side. This side included tremendous talent, such as Dalglish, Danny McGrain, Davie Hay, George Connelly and Lou Macari. Dalglish later became the bedrock of the Celtic team in the 1970's, and was a hugely influential club captain.

In November 1975 Dalglish scored a goal for Celtic against Ayr United, so stunning in its execution, that one of his contemporaries described it as *'something right out of a schoolboy comic'*. However, this was not a fictional *'Roy of the Rovers'* character in action. This was a real life hero. And to those who idolised him at that time, he was *'Kenny of the Celtic'*.

CONTENTS

Author's note: As late as 1975 some newspaper reports still referred to Kenny's surname erroneously as 'Dalgleish', but for the purpose of this book his surname will show the correct spelling at all times.

FOREWORD

There is a personal poignancy when addressing the core of Stephen Murray's excellent, informative and entertaining account of the career of Kenny Dalglish at Celtic.

A child of the fifties, I was still at primary school when Celtic won the European Cup. This did not diminish my enthusiasm for the final in Lisbon and my subsequent joy but I was more closely welded physically to later sides in that I watched them regularly as a callow recruit of the Busby and Eaglesham Supporters' Club.

If Jinky and Bobby Murdoch in particular were the love of a childhood, and one that endures in my sixties, then King Kenny – it would be insolent to call him anything else – was the hero of this young adult. In many ways, he has remained so despite his defection to Liverpool.

This book fills a substantial gap. The myth and legend of Dalglish at Liverpool has been exhaustively chronicled, rightly so given he is the club's greatest ever player and was also the manager who guided a community through Hillsborough and its awful aftermath with dignity and compassion.

But one could be forgiven for supposing that his career at Celtic was merely a prelude, the first act of a drama of extraordinary achievement.

It was much more than that, however. To those who watched him play in the Hoops, King Kenny remains an eternal monarch. He reigned with a mixture of sublime technique, substantial toughness and with an attitude that roared that football was a game to be enjoyed but it was also a contest that must be won. My overwhelming memory of him is shared by many: the arms spread wide in triumph, the cheeks spotted red with exertion and the smile denoting another goal scored, another match on the way to being won.

It is possible to argue from a modern perspective that Dalglish's transfer was inevitable. But many of us in the support then held on to the belief that it somehow might be avoided, even just delayed. After all, the Lisbon Lions all played their best football for Celtic with the practice of the club of holding on to registrations making the players powerless in attracting a move.

The culture changed, however. King Kenny, Lou Macari and David Hay were just three of the graduates from a school of talent who went on to play for English clubs. If Celtic could have held on to all three, if George Connelly had been helped to banish his demons how would the club have fared with Danny McGrain and others in the line-up?

It is a futile question, of course. It might just be the lament of that young adult in the 1970s. What is unarguable, however, is King Kenny's greatness at Celtic. I was asked by a mate in Liverpool – as the transfer was just completed – if the new recruit could replace Kevin Keegan. Football judgments are subjective but I replied vehemently and succinctly that King Kenny would eclipse all before him. It is an opinion that was vindicated but I take no pride in that. His attributes were obvious.

To watch King Kenny over an extended period at Celtic was to be educated comprehensively in his qualities. He was strong and fit, rarely succumbing to injury. He was clever with the ball, finding the correct weight and direction of pass with almost unerring precision. He could score all types of goal, from the smart finish to the spectacular shot from either foot.

He, too, gave us early intimations of his greatness. His first displays in the Hoops were a reliable indicator of what was to come.

The greatest testimony to his character and ability is that one never doubted his passion while one was regularly thrilled by a superb piece of skill under testing circumstances.

There is, though, deep sentiment among those who applauded, roared and sang in praise of and in tribute to King Kenny in those years from 1969 to 1977. It is this: there may be a wistfulness about what might have been if he had stayed but there is a heavy gratitude for what he did when he donned the green and white.

He is one of Celtic's greats. To those who never saw him at Paradise, Stephen Murray's words serve as a wonderful, revelatory exposition. To those of us who did, this book both provokes strong memories and a deep gratitude.

Hugh MacDonald

CHAPTER ONE
IN THE BEGINNING - MAY 1967

The date was 4th May 1967. Celtic assistant manager Sean Fallon sat in his car with his wife Myra and his children. It was his wedding anniversary and as a treat he was driving the family down to Ayrshire for a meal. But something was troubling Sean. He had been chasing the signature of a young footballer, the 16 year old Kenny Dalglish. However, Kenny's father Bill was not keen on his son becoming a professional footballer. He was anxious for his son to learn a trade, realising the success rate of young football players making it to professional level was not high.

Fallon had a lot on his mind. Just two days later Celtic were to visit Ibrox Park, to face Rangers in what would possibly be a league clinching game. Celtic required only one point to win their second successive league title, and had the luxury of a game in hand over Rangers should they fail to achieve their objective of winning a vital point.

There was also the small matter of Celtic's upcoming European Cup final match, against the renowned Internazionale of Milan in Lisbon. The legendary Celtic team which Jock Stein had built in two short years was approaching its zenith. The Scottish Cup, League Cup and Glasgow Cup had already been won in spectacular style, and Stein's men stood on the brink of achieving a historic clean sweep by winning every competition entered. Only the league title and European Cup remained to be won, and the next few weeks would potentially be the most important in Fallon and Stein's professional lives.

As Celtic's assistant manager, Fallon had been working hard signing some of the finest young footballers in Scotland. Tremendous prospects such as George Connelly, Davie Hay, and Lou Macari were already learning the ropes at Celtic, with older boys like Davie Cattanach and Jimmy Quinn close to a first team breakthrough. Sean's newest recruits to his growing collection of young talent were Danny McGrain, Paul Wilson and Vic Davidson.

Davidson's mother had actually sent Fallon a letter recommending her son, Victor, who was playing for amateur side, Glasgow United. Fallon was very impressed by the wording of the letter and quality of notepaper, making him curious enough to go and watch Davidson. The Celtic assistant manager took note of the young Vic, but another player also caught his eye during the game, a player by the name of Kenny Dalglish.

Glasgow United were then invited to come and play a Celtic under 16 side, under the floodlights at Celtic's Barrowfield training ground. The Glasgow United youth side were rated amongst the best in the country, and won 3-2, with Dalglish scoring one of the goals. Afterwards Fallon and Stein made enquiries about United's no 4, who had been one of the best players afield. They were surprised to learn that no Scottish club had made a move for him. Celtic had already expressed an interest in Vic Davidson and Freddie Pethard, who would both end up at Celtic Park.

Although no Scottish side had registered a formal interest in Dalglish, he had travelled to England in August 1966 for trials with Liverpool and West Ham United. At West Ham he impressed during training sessions. Harry Redknapp, then an established West Ham first team player, recalled giving the young Scot a lift to training, and described Kenny scoring a typically brilliant goal in a training game. However, the Hammers did not follow up their interest.

Kenny played a reserve game for Liverpool against Southport in the Lancashire League, and once again he performed well. He was staying in a YMCA hostel, where Liverpool representatives visited to say they were keen to have him, but Kenny thought he was too young to leave home. At this time it was normal practice for young Scottish boys to move south to English clubs after leaving school. However, by his own admission, Kenny wasn't keen to make the move south at such a tender age. He was a young man who was desperate to play football, but was also keen to remain close to home.

Eddie Gray and Peter Lorimer (both Leeds United), Asa Hartford (West Bromwich Albion) and Eddie Kelly (Arsenal) were fine examples of those from that period who toughed it out and made the breakthrough. However, the failure rate was tremendously high, and many talented young boys travelled back to Scotland thoroughly disillusioned with game, and dropped out of it altogether.

Following his trial at Liverpool Kenny was keen to return quickly to Glasgow, for good reason. He caught a train from Liverpool's Lime Street station in order to lend his support to his Rangers heroes, who were playing Celtic at Ibrox in the Glasgow Cup final. This was a time when the Glasgow Cup still attracted huge interest, and 76,456 fans turned out on a warm summer's night. They were to watch one of Celtic's greatest ever performances on the ground of their bitter rivals. The Celts romped to a 4-0 win, with Bobby Lennox scoring a spectacular hat trick. The gauntlet had been well and truly thrown down, and Celtic were aiming to continue to their dominance by harnessing the best young talent in the country.

Sometime after his appearance against Celtic's under 16 side, Sean Fallon approached Dalglish to ask if he would be interested in attending Celtic Park twice weekly, to train with Celtic's other young hopefuls. Most boys would have jumped at the opportunity, but the young Kenny was hesitant, if not reluctant. Unknown to Fallon, Kenny was a huge supporter of Rangers. The youngster still cherished the hope that Rangers would come calling for him, but although there were strong rumours of Rangers' interest, no offer was made. Kenny accepted Fallon's invite to train with the best of Celtic's young talent, but he did not have the heart to tell his father. It was left to Bill Keir, Glasgow United's manager, to inform Dalglish senior of Celtic's interest.

Which brings us to Sean Fallon's visit to the Dalglish household in Broomloan Court in May 1967. By the mid 1960's high rise flats were commonplace in Glasgow, and Broomloan Court cast its shadow over Ibrox Park, just a couple of hundred yards away. Kenny's bedroom actually overlooked Rangers' Albion training ground. At times it must have seemed that Kenny was so close to his idols that he only had to reach out to touch them.

It is imagined that Fallon initially talked football in general with Bill Dalglish. Both men were of a similar age, and must surely have waxed lyrical about the great Celtic and Rangers players of the past. They would have undoubtedly discussed the forthcoming Lisbon final. Eventually Fallon raised the idea of Kenny signing for Celtic. Realising that his son had his heart set on being a professional footballer, Kenny's father must have appreciated that this was a golden opportunity for his boy. Bill had reservations, as he wanted Kenny to have the security of a trade. However a compromise was reached, when it was agreed that Kenny should seek a trade while training and playing with Celtic on a part time basis. And, with that, Kenny Dalglish signed a provisional form and became a Celtic player.

Sean Fallon would have been delighted to have completed the signing, but would also have been well aware that it would not have been an easy decision for Bill Dalglish to make. Many a Celtic scout had been given short shrift and sent packing by fathers who would not allow their sons to sign for Celtic. Such was life within Glasgow's footballing divide of the 1960's. It is to Bill Dalglish's credit that he consented to Kenny joining Celtic. As an avid football fan he would have realised that there was no finer place for any boy to learn his trade in the game, amongst the Celtic players and management who were shortly to prove that they were the best in all of Europe.

Following the discussion with his father, Kenny is said to have gone to his room, tearing down some Rangers posters from his wall, perhaps being fearful that Fallon would notice them, take offence and change his mind regarding his signing for Celtic. He need not have worried, for it mattered not to Fallon who anyone supported. He was solely focused on the young Dalglish's ability as a footballer. It should be remembered that perhaps the greatest Celt of all, Jock Stein, was well known for having strong Rangers allegiances in his younger days and that had not held him back in his career as a Celtic player, captain and manager.

It's interesting to note that there was no financial inducement for Kenny to sign for Celtic. This is in complete contrast to the twenty first century, when youngsters are offered eye watering sums of money to sign for the major clubs. A few days after Sean Fallon's visit Kenny had the thrill of receiving his signed Celtic provisional form by post. He was on his way.

Many years later, in 2012, Kenny joined Andy Gray and Richard Keys on a Talksport radio programme, to discuss his notable career. Gray, a noted Rangers supporter from his days in Glasgow's Drumchapel, remained frustrated that Rangers had missed out on such a great talent and wanted to know how this had happened.

Gray - *How did we miss you?*

Dalglish - *Who's we?*

Gray - *Rangers!*

Dalglish - *They never asked!*

In later years, Fallon would recall in the Celtic View the evening he signed Kenny for Celtic, and commented on why he had been so keen to pursue Kenny's signature: *'The folk at Rangers thought he was too slow. A few people felt that way about Kenny at the start but I saw that he was fast in the head. Even then I was confident he could make it. He wasn't an obvious standout at that stage but he had great spirit and bravery about him and obviously loved playing the game. And right from the start he had that great balance and ability to shield the ball. I always felt he had the necessary potential.'*

If Kenny owed a debt to Sean Fallon, then he also owed as much to Myra Fallon, who sat in the car with her impatient kids for a couple of hours until Sean returned to them. She later recalled that night with some humour, especially as Kenny went on to become one of the Celtic greats.

On 25th May 1967 Celtic did indeed become European champions, when they defeated Inter Milan 2-1, playing their own brand of glorious, attacking football. There is no doubt that Dalglish senior and junior would have watched the game, televised live from Lisbon, in the comfort of their home. Perhaps Kenny dreamed of the day when he himself would take part in a game of such magnitude. Which begs a rather amusing question; did the Dalglish family, still huge Rangers fans at that time, cheer for Celtic on the night?

CHAPTER TWO

CUMBERNALD UNITED
'THE PAPER TEAM' - 1967/1968

In the summer of 1967 journalist Hugh McIlvanney commented that within European football, *'All roads lead to Celtic Park.'* The crown of European Champions belonged to Celtic following their momentous triumph in Lisbon. Celtic didn't just beat Inter Milan, they annihilated them, and the 2-1 scoreline did not reflect Celtic's superiority on the night. These were heady times, days which Celtic fans and the city of Glasgow would never experience again. It's worth pointing out that shortly after Celtic's victory in Lisbon, Rangers travelled to Nuremberg to play Bayern Munich in the European Cup Winners Cup final. They were defeated by the narrow margin of 1-0. To have two Glasgow teams in major European finals in the same season represented a great sporting achievement for the city, unmatched to this day.

As European Champions, Celtic were honoured to receive an invitation from Real Madrid, to play in Alfredo Di Stefano's testimonial match. The game was not purely for the great Di Stefano's financial benefit, but also to let the sporting world know that Real were in fact still Europe's masters. Although these Scottish interlopers had won the European premier competition they were still considered inferior by the mighty Real, who had won six of the previous eleven tournaments.

To accept the challenge would mean Celtic gambling with their newly won reputation. A defeat would leave them open to much criticism. When Jock Stein asked his players if they wished to play in the game, every one of them gave a resounding *'yes'*. They would have relished the prospect of playing for the legendary *'Blonde Arrow'*, and the opportunity of performing in the grand setting of the Bernabeau stadium. Stein allowed himself the liberty of making one change to his team, with reserve goalkeeper John Fallon replacing Ronnie Simpson. Perhaps his reasoning was that Celtic could claim the team selection wasn't their full Lisbon eleven, should they be beaten in Madrid.

As it happened, Celtic won 1-0 on the night, with Fallon playing magnificently. Jimmy Johnstone gave a wondrous display, capturing the hearts of the Madrid public, who gave him shouts of, *'Ole!'*, as the wee man tortured Real defenders time after time with his magnificent dribbling skills. Celtic won the European Cup in Lisbon. In Madrid they became the undisputed champions of Europe.

For Kenny Dalglish, turning up at Celtic Park for pre-season training in that glorious era, there must have been a tremendous feeling of exhilaration. For a sixteen year old boy to join any professional club would have been an exciting prospect, but to join the European Cup holders would surely have been an impossible dream come true for any youngster.

Kenny was indeed a very fortunate boy. As a Rangers supporter he had watched the great Rangers side of the early 1960's, arguably the greatest Rangers team of all time. Supporters of the period could easily name their heroes, from one to eleven, as team line ups rarely changed then. The Rangers team of Ritchie, Shearer and Caldow, Greig, McKinnon and Baxter, Henderson, McMillan and Miller, Brand and Wilson was one of the finest sides ever to grace the Scottish game.

Having won the domestic Scottish treble in 1964, Rangers looked set to make their mark in the European Cup, but the football gods deemed to intervene. In December 1964 they travelled to Austria to play Rapid Vienna, holding a slender 1-0 lead from the first leg. In Vienna the influential Jim Baxter helped Rangers to a deserved 2-0 victory on a frozen pitch. Unfortunately, late in the game a Rapid defender took retribution on *'Slim Jim'*, with a horrendous tackle which broke Baxter's leg. This European tie had an afternoon kick off and was shown live on television, a very rare event back then, with the young Kenny able to watch his team emerge triumphant.

In the quarter finals, Rangers, without their talisman Fifer, lost 3-2 on aggregate to Inter Milan, who then went on to win the trophy. A few weeks later Jock Stein moved from Hibernian to manage Celtic, and the balance of power within Scottish football changed completely. During the next ten years Stein would take Celtic to a level of glory their fans could barely have dreamed of.

In the mid 1980's Jim Baxter courted controversy in the Evening Times, by claiming that the fine Rangers side of the early 1960's were a better side than Celtic's Lisbon Lions of 1967. Bertie Auld, ever the defender of Celtic, was given the right of reply, and ended the debate by responding in his own inimitable way; *'Jim knows where I stay. He can come over here anytime and I'll show him medals he's never seen!'*

Kenny Dalglish had been weaned on the fine Rangers side of the early 1960's, and it was said that his playing style was reminiscent of Rangers' inside right Ian McMillan, nicknamed, *'the wee prime minister'*. McMillan was a beautifully balanced player, who made up a midfield duet with the unique Baxter, in the days of the popular 4-2-4 formation. Now, Dalglish turned up at Celtic Park to train and learn from players who were rightly regarded as the best on the continent.

When he arrived at Celtic Kenny played in the right half position, and would possibly have been considered a potential understudy for the great Bobby Murdoch, regarded by many as the greatest of the Lisbon Lions. Murdoch was Celtic's midfield playmaker, a wonderful passer of the ball, whether it was the short variety or the raking forty yard pass. He was a marvellous combination of hard tackler and expert of subtle flicks and touches, which could prise open the tightest of defences. Bobby was a master craftsman, and the young Kenny would now be seen as his apprentice.

Stein and Fallon were amassing a wonderful group of young players, who would be bestowed with the nickname of *'The Quality Street Gang'*, a moniker given because of their individual and collective talent. There was also quality in the Celtic scouting system, headed by Sean Fallon. However, even this fine Celtic youth system allowed a couple of gems slip through the net. Jim Holton and Graeme Souness, both Scotland World Cup players of the future, trained with Celtic during this period but weren't pursued any further.

Jim Craig, Celtic's right back in their European Cup winning team, would later recall giving lifts to Kenny Dalglish, Danny McGrain and Graeme Souness. He humorously claimed that it was his advice on those journeys which inspired them to be the great players they became.

On 20th July 1967 Jock Stein took thirty six players for a three hour long pre-season work out. Press photographs were taken for posterity, showing the players with Stein, Sean Fallon, Neilly Mochan and Bob Rooney. A very youthful Kenny Dalglish, face flushed from his earlier exertions, can be seen sitting proudly in the front row. The Lisbon Lions' squad all featured, alongside the new recruits, in what is undeniably the finest collection of footballers ever seen in Scottish football. Celtic captain, Billy McNeill, recalled those days in an Evening Times feature: *'Big Jock used to bring in schoolboys and allow them to train with the rest of the lads. I remember Kenny distinctly because he was so outstanding. I took an interest in him. He had chubby little cheeks which went a delightful shade of red when he was exerting himself and he was invariably doing that.'*

After signing young players provisionally, Celtic's policy was to farm them out to play for teams in the Scottish junior leagues. This was a successful practice which the club operated for many years. The rationale was for the boys to play organised football against mature players. The junior game had a reputation for being rugged and lacking in sophistication, and it was a learning curve which was designed to toughen up the boys in preparation for graduation to the senior game.

At the start of season 1967-68, Celtic arranged for Kenny to visit junior side Cumbernauld United. Celtic official, Frank Meechan, took him to see the set up at Cumbernauld. Kenny played two highly successful trial games. In the second game he scored four goals against Yoker Athletic. It was then agreed that he would play for Cumbernauld for the season, in a move which would be mutually beneficial to both Kenny and Cumbernauld.

Kenny found employment as an apprentice joiner, as his father desired. However, he also continued to train with the other young hopefuls at Celtic Park, in addition to training with Cumbernauld. The junior side saw him as a replacement for Johnny Hamilton, who had moved up to the senior game, signing for Hibernian. Hamilton went on to enjoy a successful career at senior level.

Cumbernauld was a bustling and expanding 'new town', which had been created in the 1950's to accommodate the population overspill from Glasgow. The residents of Cumbernauld were keen to start a football team to play in the Scottish junior league, and a committee was formed for this purpose in 1964. They worked to establish a new club, named Cumbernauld United. It was slow progress initially, as funds had to be raised to purchase land for the team to play on. The new Cumbernauld club were eventually accepted into the junior ranks, to play in Junior League Division B in season 1967-68.

It was proposed that United should play in claret and blue. This was the suggestion of committee member Frank Keene, who was a fervent West Ham fan. The new club adopted the Hammers' colours, which they have kept until present day. West Ham, in fact, were said to have donated the first set of strips as a goodwill gesture to the new junior club now playing in their famed claret and blue.

Kenny Dalglish was an immediate hit for Cumbernauld, and his fine form did not go unnoticed, when after only a few weeks at the club he was chosen to play in a trial match for a Scottish junior select side. Celtic continued to keep tabs on their new boy's progress over the season, but it's interesting to note that Kenny's switch of allegiance from Rangers' blue to Celtic's green was not an immediate one.

On 30th August 1967 Celtic played Rangers at Parkhead in a vital League Cup tie, in the old four team group format. This was the deciding fixture in the group, and victory for either side would guarantee a place in the quarter finals. Although it was still very early in the season, a win would have been a huge morale boost for the victors, and a major blow for the losers. A massive crowd of 94,168 packed Ibrox for the first game between the teams, an attendance which could not be matched by any other British fixture. This was a clear indication of the pulling power that Glasgow's big two had at the time. The match ended in a 1-1 draw.

The attendance for the Celtic Park decider was 75,000. Many fans may also recall this evening for another reason. The final episode of 'The Fugitive' was to be shown on television, presenting fans with the dilemma of whether to go to the game or watch the culmination of a favourite TV show, with videotape technology being some way off.

Rangers were leading 1-0 when they were awarded a penalty in the 76th minute, with Tommy Gemmell sending Willie Henderson sprawling in the penalty area. As young Celtic players, Kenny

Dalglish and Danny McGrain were sitting together in the main stand watching developments on the field of play. Kai Johansen took the ensuing penalty. He crashed his shot off the cross bar and then headed the rebound at Celtic's goalkeeper, Ronnie Simpson, thus giving Celtic a free kick. As Danny McGrain leapt to his feet with delight, Kenny could be seen slumped in his seat in disappointment at Johansen's miss. Celtic took advantage of this good fortune, and in the last 12 minutes went into overdrive, scoring three times to emerge victorious by 3-1. This was a landmark victory for Jock Stein's Celtic side. Celtic fans, though mentally drained, remained long after the final whistle singing their songs of victory - *'We are the team in Scotland...we shall not be moved!'*

At this stage young Kenny may have been a Celtic player, but his heart was most certainly still with Rangers. As late as March 1968 he attended Ibrox to watch Rangers play Leeds United in the Fairs Cup. The game was beamed live from Elland Road and shown on a huge screen.

Cumbernauld's inaugural season was turning out to be a an exciting one, with the young Dalglish coming very much to the fore. The team were playing at St Patrick's pitch in Kilsyth until work on their new ground at Ravenswood was complete, although things didn't always go according to plan. Cumbernauld United's manager, Bob Woods, had agreed to purchase some old railway sleepers from British Rail to construct a small terracing around the Ravenswood pitch. He arranged for a group of volunteers to collect them. Unfortunately they mistakenly took the wrong sleepers, so had to replace them as requested by British Rail.

The main reason Kenny joined Cumbernauld, rather than any other junior side, was that Bob Woods and Jock Stein were good friends. Stein knew that his young protégé would be in good hands with Woods and the Cumbernauld set up. Jock was a big fan of junior football and had great admiration for the *'football people'* who ran it. This was real grass roots football, with junior teams run in the main by groups of volunteers who cut grass, cleaned dressing rooms, and lined the pitch. Bob Woods was a classic example of this, demonstrated by his huge enthusiasm and dedication to the cause of Cumbernauld United.

Eric Drever, a Cumbernauld supporter from the club's earliest days, recalls Kenny Dalglish making an immediate impression in his new surroundings: *'I have a pen pal in Cornwall, who believe it or not I still write to, and I wrote to him back then to say keep an eye out for the name, Kenny Dalglish, and he still reminds me of it now. We got a few Celtic players around then such as Tommy Livingstone, who was a goalkeeper, and Freddie Pethard. Kenny played as an attacking inside forward, and we had another inside man, Albert 'Abie' Monaghan, who I thought was a better prospect than Kenny because he was bigger and stronger. Abie went professional with Hibs but he sadly didn't make it at Easter Road. But him and Kenny were great together for that season.'*

Cumbernauld were making steady progress in the league, but the main excitement of the season came in the Scottish Junior Cup, as Eric recalls: *'We reached the fifth round of the Scottish Cup and played Johnstone Burgh at Adamslie Park in Kirkintilloch, which was a 1-1 draw in front of 8,000 people. The game was played in Kirkintilloch as our ground in Ravenswood wasn't ready, and the second game was a 2-2 draw at Johnstone, where Kenny got injured. He couldn't play in the third game, which was back in Adamslie, and we lost 1-0. I still think if Kenny had been fit we could have won the cup that year, as Johnstone Burgh went on to beat Kilsyth Rangers in the final in 1968. We were a sensation in the first season. We had all our players kitted out in blazers and slacks and the rest of the league called us 'The Paper Team' as we were never out of the newspapers. We got a lot of publicity and were doing well.'*

During the course of the season the young Dalglish made a few headlines of his own, by scoring 37 goals. Perhaps his best performance came against Cambuslang Rangers, a noted junior side of the period, when he scored a hat trick. This was an achievement in itself, but it was the variety of the goals that left an impression on Eric Drever: *'For goal one he beat a couple of players before scoring, another one was a header and the third one was a shot from outside the area. This showed he could score a variety of goals and that he had all the attributes to play at a higher level and he was still only 17 years old.'*

Cumbernauld United finished in fourth place in Division B, a huge achievement for a club playing in their first season. There was an added bonus, when due to league reconstruction, fourth place was deemed enough to merit promotion to Division A. The Cumbernauld committee had worked tirelessly on their new ground at Ravenswood. Their relationship with Celtic was to come to full fruition when Jock Stein agreed to Bob Woods' request to bring a Celtic team to Cumbernauld for the grand opening of the new ground. Cumbernauld's expectations were then exceeded, when on the evening of 13th May 1968 Jock Stein brought the full Celtic team to play at Ravenswood. Only days previously Celtic had clinched their third consecutive league title under Stein's reign. They were also technically still European champions, prior to Manchester United playing Benfica at Wembley in the 1968 European Cup final.

There were two games for the spectators to enjoy on the night. The Celtic first eleven played Cumbernauld United in two halves of fifteen minutes, with Celtic winning 2-0. Bobby Lennox had the privilege of scoring the first goal on the new Ravenswood pitch, with Willie Wallace scoring the other. The Celtic side was Simpson, Gemmell and O'Neill; Murdoch, McNeill and Brogan; Johnstone, Gallagher and Wallace; Lennox and Hughes. In the second game a Celtic second eleven beat United 4-1, with goals from Lou Macari (2), George Connelly and Jimmy Quinn. The team line up was Wraith Murray and Gorman; Cattanach, McKellar and Hogg; Murdoch (Billy), Connelly and Quinn; Macari and Clark.

Kenny Dalglish played for United against his soon to be Celtic team mates, and a photograph was taken for posterity. It shows the Celtic stars happily lining up alongside the United players and officials, with a young Kenny in the front row, squeezed between Bobby Murdoch and Willie Wallace.

The excitement of the evening is still fondly remembered by the Cumbernauld officials, as Eric Drever recalls: *'Around 5,000 people squeezed in to the old place that night. There were young boys climbing on roofs, anything to get a good vantage point. We couldn't believe it when Stein sent the first team and this was greatly appreciated as we thought he would have played a reserve team. We made a lot of money on the night which was invested back into the club.'*

Stein assisted with the ceremonial cutting of the ribbon beforehand, and the festivities continued after the match. A reception for players, officials and guests took place in the Masonic hall in Cumbernauld village. A meal which quaintly included *'green and white onions'* was served, and Jock Stein was presented with a special pennant by the club. The Celtic officials were given a small trophy to commemorate the event. Bob Woods said: *'Bringing Celtic to Cumbernauld is unique within the history of Scottish junior football. No team has ever been so ambitious and I doubt if another match like this will ever be seen again.'*

In later years Cumbernauld United continued their cordial relationship with Celtic, as Eric Drever describes: *'We actually played a game at Celtic Park in a Scottish Cup replay against Kirkintilloch Rob Roy in 1971. There were two draws and Sean Fallon came here to see the second game. Afterwards we were discussing a neutral venue for the third match, when Sean said he would arrange for it to be played at Parkhead. It was a great night and we won 4-2 in front of a crowd of 13,000. Celtic were very good to us at that time. I remember once at Kilsyth, Jock Stein was standing in the crowd with the punters, not for him going to the committee rooms or the pavilions to watch. In these days the entertainment at junior games was terrific and we drew big crowds.'*

Young Kenny showed great aptitude in learning his footballing trade at Cumbernauld, but the same couldn't be said of his prowess at joinery work. In interviews over the years he remarked humorously that he spent his time, *'shovelling shavings and hitting nails - mostly my own.'* He also found having to go straight to training from work in the evenings very demanding. His heart was set on playing football for a living and he had no interest in being a joiner.

Cumbernauld were extremely keen for Kenny to return to Ravenswood for another season, and Jock Stein was said to be receptive to this. However, Kenny and Danny McGrain were both so desperate to go full time at Celtic that they visited the Celtic manager to present their case. While Dalglish had enjoyed a modicum of success at Cumbernauld, McGrain, in comparison, had experienced a difficult time at Maryhill Juniors, who had hardly won a match. Stein was said to have given them a sympathetic hearing, and made arrangements for their fathers to come to Parkhead to discuss their futures.

In May 1967 Sean Fallon was required to use all of his powers of persuasion to talk Bill Dalglish into permitting Kenny to join Celtic. Now one year on, it was Bill's turn to attempt to persuade Stein that it was in everyone's best interests for Kenny to sign as a full time player at Parkhead, and to concentrate fully on his football career. Stein knew of the hunger and desire that Dalglish had to make the grade, and eventually acceded to this request. Kenny Dalglish then signed a contract and became a full time Celtic player, meaning that there would be no more laborious joinery work. Danny McGrain was to comment later that had he and Kenny respectively became an engineer and joiner then, *'there would be bridges and shelves falling down all over Scotland. Our hearts just weren't in it.'*

There was one more footballing commitment for Kenny to fulfil before the end of the season. Celtic had been invited to send a team to play in the prestigious Casale Monferrato youth tournament in

Italy. Casale Monferrato is a town in the north of the country, near Turin, and the tournament was described as a *'junior European Cup.'* Celtic sent a squad of nineteen of their best young players. Before travelling they were kitted out at a Glasgow tailors with their smart new blazers, complete with the Celtic crest. This was a source of great pride and many of them in later years would comment on their excitement at receiving official Celtic apparel, and the anticipation of flying out to a foreign land to play football. It's reckoned that none of the boys had flown before, so there was a great sense of adventure amongst those who travelled. The Celtic squad were given great publicity in the press, who published a wonderful photograph of the young Celts outside Glasgow airport, literally leaping in the air with excitement.

On 31st May 1968 the Celtic squad flew out to Italy. They were goalkeepers - Bobby Wraith and Tommy Livingstone; outfield players - John Murray (vice captain), Danny McGrain, John Gorman, Freddie Pethard, Jackie Clarke, George Connelly (captain), Billy Murdoch, Paul Wilson, David Hay, Kenny Dalglish, Tony McBride, Pat McMahon, Johnny Hemphill, Lou Macari, Hugh McKellar, Jim Clark and Victor Davidson. The party were chaperoned by Sean Fallon and Celtic physio, Bob Rooney.

The trip was to prove a great experience for the young Celts. As carefree young boys there was an element of high spirits, although no one overstepped the mark. Celtic were placed in a four team group with Juventus, Sparta Prague and local Italian side, AS Casale Calcio. In their three games the boys made a great impression on the locals, with their fine play winning the journalists award for the most entertaining side. Sadly, their good performances gained no reward. Following a narrow 1-0 defeat to Juventus, their remaining two games ended in goalless draws, leaving the Celts out of the tournament.

There were two underlying problems which the young Celtic

players faced. The first was playing on the hard baked ground, in stifling heat they were not used to. The other matter was that due to an administrative error, Celtic were under the misapprehension they were to play in an under 19 tournament, when it was actually for players under 21. This meant that the boys gave away a couple of years to the other teams, which was said to have been a considerable disadvantage for them. Kenny Dalglish was one of the youngest players in the party, having just turned 17 years old, and did not play in any of the three matches. In spite of the results the tournament was deemed as being a great success for the development of the Celtic boys. Casale Monferatto had given them a taste of what to expect in the future, were they to be successful, and in later years they were to look back on their Italian adventures with a great deal of fondness.

....

The Celtic View illustrates Celtic's growing popularity, following their European success.

> The Celtic Story Film will be shown again in Toronto on Tuesday April 16th in the Eaton Auditorium and on April 26th the film goes for its first showing in the Montreal area to the Verdun Catholic High School Auditorium.

Celtic View 16th April 1968

....

CHAPTER THREE
APPRENTICESHIP - 1968/1969

In the spring of 1968 Celtic won their third consecutive League title under Jock Stein. It had been by far the closest and most exhilarating title race to date, with Rangers pushing all the way in a gripping climax to the season. Rangers held the advantage after the New Year, and by early February led Celtic by six points, with Celtic having two games in hand. Rangers remained ahead throughout February and March, but by the start of April their lead over Celtic was just one point, with four games remaining. The tide turned on the night of 17th April, when lowly Morton held Rangers in a dramatic 3-3 draw at Cappielow. This meant that Celtic and Rangers were level on 59 points, with Celtic having a considerable goal difference advantage of 21. Only two games were left to play.

Morton had clearly taken confidence from the Rangers result, and when they came to Parkhead three days later they defended for their lives for over ninety minutes, almost ruining Celtic's title hopes in the process. With only seconds remaining, Bobby Lennox prodded in the winning goal during a goalmouth scramble, giving Celtic a 2-1 win and sending the 51,000 crowd delirious with joy. When the final whistle blew just seconds later Jock Stein raced on to the pitch to embrace the popular Lennox, knowing full well the importance of his goal.

Rangers chose to play their final match against Aberdeen at Ibrox on Scottish Cup final day, 27th April, when Hearts would face

Dunfermline Athletic at Hampden Park. This decision saw the Ibrox club receive a great deal of criticism, as it was felt that this would affect the attendance at Hampden for what was Scottish football's showpiece match. Celtic had a free day, as they had been due to play Dunfermline. This match had been rescheduled for 30th April. Rangers hoped to gain advantage by playing their own fixture prior to this date.

Stein publicly encouraged the Celtic fans to turn out at Hampden to boost the gate, and on the day a respectable crowd of 56,000 attended. He set an example by bringing the entire Celtic squad to the final to lend their weight to the occasion, but he also used the opportunity to spy on Athletic in preparation for Celtic's final game of the season. Dunfermline defeated Hearts 3-1. After the final whistle Stein approached his players to joyfully regale them with the news that Aberdeen had sensationally beaten Rangers 3-2 at Ibrox, courtesy of an Ian Taylor goal, with only two minutes remaining. Astonishingly, this was Rangers first league defeat, in their final game of the season. The pressure had eventually told on the Ibrox club and they had cracked.

There had been signs as far back as March that Rangers were feeling the strain. At that time they were still in the running for four competitions. They were due to meet Celtic in a Glasgow Cup semi final but pulled out of the fixture, claiming they had an overload of matches to play in the League, Scottish Cup and the European Inter Cities Fairs Cup. Celtic then received a bye into the final, where they defeated Clyde 8-0. Rangers' decision led to accusations that they were afraid to play Celtic, who were now in a rich vein of form, and a victory at this time would have given Celtic a considerable psychological advantage for the League run in. Observers also pointed out that Celtic had been in exactly the same position regarding fixture congestion just twelve months previously, and had gone on to win every competition. The Celtic fans gleefully taunted their rivals by singing, *'The Huns are feart tae play us, and so say all of us!'* until the end of the season.

As it happened Rangers lost to Hearts in the Scottish Cup quarter final, were defeated by Leeds United in Europe and allowed Celtic to snatch the League title from their grasp, leaving them without a trophy. On 30th April Celtic travelled to East End Park knowing that only a 23-0 defeat would stop them achieving three in a row. A record attendance of over 27,000 crowded into Dunfermline's tight ground that night, with thousands more locked outside. There was a party atmosphere as Dunfermline paraded their newly won Scottish Cup trophy. Jock Stein was said to be particularly delighted as he still had a great deal of affection for Dunfermline, who had given him his first job as a manager in 1960. During the match spectator safety was of paramount importance, with the game being stopped several times for staff to coax fans down from the enclosure roof and from floodlights, where they were endangering themselves and others around them. Celtic won 2-1 through two Bobby Lennox goals, to finish the season in style.

In winning the title Celtic created some remarkable records. They established a League record by attaining 63 points, scoring an incredible 106 goals in the process and losing only 24. Their unbeaten run had begun in September, culminating with the team winning their last 16 fixtures. The Celts also created another Scottish League record, by winning 16 consecutive away games. The outstanding Bobby Lennox scored 32 goals in just 28 league games, scoring 23 times in the final 12 games of the season. All in all, a fantastic achievement by all concerned.

Kenny Dalglish and the other young Celtic players turned up for pre-season training in the summer of 1968 with a manager and a group of players who had now reached legendary status. Lou Macari, who was already on the Celtic ground staff, remembers the excitement of those early days: '*You were in awe of being there and in awe of the first team players. There was no conversation, you just looked at them.*'

Although the youngest members of the squad held the Celtic players in the highest regard, the experienced Celts of the period were a very supportive group. They gladly gave their time, and readily shared advice and experience with the youngsters training and working alongside them. Kenny recalled this later in the Celtic View: *'The one thing that was really obvious from the very first day, when I was only sixteen, was the humility of the players. They never dismissed any of the younger boys that trained alongside them. Pre-season everybody trained together, and obviously when the season started they would go and do their training and we would do ours, but they never ever undermined you. They'd have a laugh and joke with you and if you were standing waiting for a bus they'd give you a run into town.'*

Kenny also commented that turning up for training with the Lisbon Lions was, *'like playing in a cup final every day.'* It was only natural that he and the other young lads would be apprehensive, but in the main they were trained by Willie Fernie, who was said to have had a tremendous influence on the *'Quality Street Gang'* of that time. Fernie's coaching methods were both effective, enjoyable and said to be ahead of their time. Two touch football was encouraged, as well as the use of one-two's, with everything geared to the stylish, attacking football for which Celtic were now famed.

Fernie had been a tremendous Celtic player in the 1950s, and was the major influence in Celtic's legendary 7-1 League Cup Final thrashing of Rangers in 1957. He was a creative, stylish inside forward, and Jock Stein encouraged his old team mate to educate the young players in the method of attacking football for which the team had become renowned. Fernie's young charges would also learn about discipline in this new Celtic reserve set up. Punctuality was expected at all times and long hair or facial hair would not be tolerated, even in the more liberal times of the late 1960s.

Happily for Kenny Dalglish, he made an immediate impression on the senior players. Bobby Lennox, for one, being impressed: *'Right from the start from when he walked into Parkhead we knew he'd be something special. When he joined in at training - and remember this was our European Cup winning team - he was never overawed. He had so much class that he never looked out of place.'*

At this stage in his career Kenny had been earmarked to play as a right half, in the no 4 shorts, which in those days was the role of an attacking midfield player. Billy McNeill remembers: *'At first Kenny didn't play as a forward. He was in midfield. I always felt he could play anywhere as he always had awareness and assurance. I used to pick him up in the mornings on the way to training. He was a very refreshing bloke because he didn't drink. He was very conscientious.'*

Celtic's pre-season training under Neilly Mochan and Willie Fernie was overseen by both Jock Stein and Sean Fallon. Fitness was a prerequisite for any Celtic side under Stein, and there was a pride in the level of fitness that players had achieved since Stein's arrival in 1965. There was no doubting the talent of the players at Celtic Park, but Stein appreciated that a high level of fitness would be a distinct advantage to his team, and this proved to be the case in 1968 when Rangers wilted in the run in, enabling Celtic to take the league title. Training was hard but Stein and his coaches made it as enjoyable as possible. The senior players were said to be hard workers in training, setting a fine example to the youngsters, whom they influenced greatly.

In these early days Kenny would meet fellow reserve player, Danny McGrain, on the number 64 bus from Glasgow city centre to Celtic Park. They had known each other from Glasgow schoolboy select teams and would become firm friends for the rest of their Celtic days. Although this was an exciting time, Kenny must have been feeling some pressure. Firstly to do well at Cumbernauld United; then to do well in training at Barrowfield; now to do well for the Celtic reserves.

On Wednesday August 19th Kenny played in a young Celtic select, which lost 5-4 in a friendly against to Morton at Cappielow. In the club's official weekly newspaper, the Celtic View, the new squad photograph was printed. Young Kenny featured, kitted out in the Celts' all green change strip. He was sandwiched between the experienced duo of John Clark and Willie O'Neill. The Celtic View at this time was the only weekly club newspaper in Britain. It had an impressive weekly circulation of between 25,000 and 30,000, and was sent to Celtic fans all over the world.

Kenny made an impression against Morton, and was named at right half for the reserves' first league game of the season, against Dundee United at Parkhead. The young Celts won 4-1, with goals from Joe McBride(2), Lou Macari and Jim Clarke. The Celtic team was - Wraith, Craig and Gorman; Dalglish, Clarke and Clark; Wilson, McBride and Chalmers; Macari and Clarke. The substitute was Danny McGrain.

Lisbon Lions Jim Craig, John Clark and Steve Chalmers all featured in the side, which also included Joe McBride. Jock Stein was a great believer in playing experienced players amongst the younger element of his reserve teams. An *'old head'* could pass on his experience on the field of play, without a manager having to bark instructions from the sidelines, and the more mature players could also teach youngsters good habits, which would stay with them for the rest of their careers.

....

A letter from a rival supporter commends *'old head'* Ronnie Simpson on his performance against Rangers. It was published in Jimmy Hill's Soccer Weekly in September 1968, following Celtic's 2-0 win.

Sir - Through your magazine I would like to pay tribute to a brilliant goalkeeper. It was during the recent Rangers v Celtic game at Ibrox, and Celtic had a two goal lead at half time. But after half time, Rangers hammered Celtic, brilliant shots came in from all angles but this 'keeper would not be beaten. Then a cross came in from the left - Smith, Rangers' inside-right ran forward, jumped and met it thigh high. It was a tremendous shot but the 'keeper, with tremendous reflexes, punched it over the bar. The goalkeeper was Ronnie Simpson, the old man of Celtic. I'm sure he'll never have another game like it. Without him Celtic would have been thrashed. This was a goalkeeping display better than anything I saw in the World Cup. AND I'm a Rangers supporter!

R Bisland , Glasgow

....

In August 1968 the Celtic reserve team were in a three team reserve League Cup group, with Rangers and Partick Thistle. One team would qualify for the quarter finals of the tournament. On 31st August Celtic faced Partick Thistle at home in their final group game, knowing they required to win by a considerable margin to advance to the next round. Lou Macari remembered this game in an Evening Times special feature: *'We needed to beat Partick Thistle by seven clear goals to win the section we were in. Sean Fallon was managing us and he said 'Right, this is a mammoth task. You're on £25 a man.' Normally we got £1.50 for a win, £25 was nearly a week's wages. We were wetting ourselves with excitement.'* This game was one of Kenny Dalglish's earliest appearances in a Celtic jersey, and he was part of a team performance which would become part of Celtic folklore, as Macari remembers: *'We were 6-0 up at half time and we won 12-0. That was a match which summed the team up.'*

The scorers that day were Joe McBride (4), Lou Macari (4), Bertie Auld (2) and Paul Wilson (2). The Celtic team fielded that day has been described as the finest reserve side ever to have represented the club: Ronnie Simpson, Danny McGrain and John Gorman; Kenny

Dalglish, David Hay and John Clark; Paul Wilson, Pat McMahon and Joe McBride, Lou Macari and Bertie Auld. The substitute was Hugh McKellar.

This was such a remarkable result that Rangers' Alex Miller, a reserve player at the time, recalled his team mates assumed that the Evening Times had misprinted the scoreline, never believing that Celtic could win by such a margin. Miller would later discover that drubbings from this Celtic reserve team were not unusual. Even Jock Stein was said to have been taken aback when he discovered how well his reserve side had played.

Celtic fan, Brian McKenzie, a relation of Joe McBride, recalls Joe telling a story about this game in later life: '*Joe was coming back from injury in 1968 and was playing with the reserves. Jock Stein asked him to keep an eye on young Kenny in one of his early appearances and to give him his opinion. After the game Joe told Jock he wasn't that impressed and that he couldn't see much in him. Years later the family used to pull Joe's leg about that, and they joked this was the reason he went into the pub game and not into football management.*'

Kenny may not have made a great impression on Joe McBride but, more importantly, he had impressed Sean Fallon, who reported in the Celtic View: '*A subtle blend of youth and experience won this match....Kenny Dalglish is making his mark at right half. The 17 year old had two really good games against Dundee United and Partick Thistle, and yet he is only one of the potentially great teenagers we have at Parkhead.*'

The first Old Firm league game of the season was always a keenly anticipated affair, even at reserve level. On 14th September Celtic reserves travelled the short distance to Ibrox, although Kenny was not with them. As he lived in the high flats adjacent to Ibrox, it made no sense for him to travel to Celtic Park as would have been normal practice, and Sean Fallon had agreed to Kenny's request to meet the team outside Ibrox. When the reserves arrived some of the players mentioned to Kenny that Jock Stein had been looking for him before they had left. This concerned Kenny as he had no idea as to why Stein should have been looking for him. Kenny played at Ibrox in the no 6 shorts at left half, in what was said to have been a physical encounter. Rangers played a number of out of favour first team men such as Erik Sorensen, Bobby Watson, Kai Johansen, Alex Smith and a certain Alex Ferguson.

'Fergie', as the media loved to refer to him, would later become a knight of the realm, but at this point he was having a difficult time at Ibrox and was languishing in the reserves. In later years, when both men had become outstanding, successful football managers, Kenny and Alex would recall this encounter fondly, with somewhat differing views. Dalglish recalled that Celtic easily thwarted Ferguson's aggressive style of play, while Alex claimed that he scored in a Rangers victory. The facts show that Celtic won 1-0, through a goal by the prolific Joe McBride.

On returning to training the following Monday morning, Dalglish was a bit apprehensive as to why Jock Stein had been looking for him before the game at Ibrox. Stein informed Kenny that he had only wanted to give him a word of encouragement, recognising he may have been nervous about playing in his first Old Firm encounter for Celtic, especially at Ibrox. Stein himself had come from a strong Rangers background and this incident showed that he had an understanding of the situation, and was sensitive to the feelings of one of his youngest players. Perhaps this was finally the day when Kenny left any lingering Rangers allegiance behind him and became a fully adopted Celt.

....

While Kenny played in the reserves, Celtic fans taunted the Rangers support about their expensive new signings, Dave and Alex Smith. They sang the following when Celtic eliminated their rivals from the League Cup in August 1968.

Oh they paid a hundred thoosand for the Smiths

Oh they paid a hundred thoosand for the Smiths

Oh they paid a hundred thoosand

And the b******s kept on losin'

Oh they paid a hundred thoosand for the Smiths

....

One week after playing at Ibrox Kenny surprisingly found himself dropped from the reserve team against Dunfermline, with Sean Fallon informing the Celtic View: *'Kenny Dalglish got the day off on Saturday but I know the boy won't be too disappointed. He is a highly promising youngster but such is the strength of our playing staff we can afford to nurse him along to full maturity. Kenny won't be long on the touchline.'*

However, it appears that Fallon had an ulterior motive for leaving Kenny out. On 25th September Celtic travelled to Douglas Park to play Hamilton Accies in a League Cup quarter final second leg tie, holding a massive 10-0 lead from the first game. Much to Kenny's surprise, he was named as substitute for the this game, and a potential first team appearance after only a few weeks at the club as a full timer. Jock Stein had left Fallon in charge of the Celtic side while he travelled south to watch the Carlisle United v Leicester City League Cup tie. Newspapers reported that he was there to cast his eye over two potential signings, Alan Ross, the Carlisle goalkeeper and Davie Gibson, Leicester's Scottish inside forward.

Youngsters Bobby Wraith and John Gorman made the headlines, as it was announced they would make their first team debuts. However, there had been no advance warning of Kenny being in the squad. Kenny took the field for his first team debut when he replaced Charlie Gallagher in the second half. He appeared to have made an impression on Hugh Taylor of the Daily Record: *'And what a difference this Dalglish kid made, adding power and punch to Celtic, who began to speed it up, much to the consternation of the Accies' defence.'* Celtic's young team equipped itself well and ran out 4-2 winners on the night.

Afterwards Stein made no apology for playing a so called weakened side. He told the Celtic View: *'I know officialdom will criticise me for playing so many of my youngsters in this game, pointing out that it is my duty to field a full strength side. It is also my duty to see that Celtic maintain their high standard and position in Scottish football. Officialdom cannot have the best of both worlds. Such is the demand on our players for international matches that we can only find out who are the best possible stand-ins for injured stars by seeing the boys in action. That's the reason I selected this side for that cup-tie.'*

Sadly for fellow debutants Wraith and Gorman, this would be their only competitive Celtic appearance, before moving on to pastures new. However, it appears that the young Dalglish was as keen to make as good an impression off the pitch as he had done on it, as Celtic goalkeeper John Fallon recalls: *'Kenny was a very quiet, shy boy and I remember being surprised when he came to my house one day. I had a pal called Jim Coogan who was a bespoke tailor in Hamilton and I used to get my suits from him. I took Kenny out to Jim for his first bespoke suit, a fashionable suit, he was only 18 years old and had not long arrived from Cumbernauld United.'*

Kenny had made a real name for himself by appearing in a first team game, but he knew that there was a long way to go. It was Stein's policy to give young players a wee taster in the senior side, and then put them back in the reserves to continue their development. As Kenny dropped back into reserve team football, Celtic overcame their first hurdle in the European Cup. French champions, St Etienne, won 2- 0 in France. However they capitulated at Celtic Park , and were defeated 4-0.

....

Mr Michael Doyle of Glasgow has informed us that Celtic's game tonight with Saint Etienne in France will be on the radio - in French. The broadcast will be on 1850 metres on the long wave band and should be picked up with reasonable reception on most wireless sets. Celtic followers need not be put off listening to commentary because of the language barrier, as many words like 'goal' are pronounced almost exactly the same as in English. Mr Doyle suggests that you keep your radio as far away from the TV set as possible as this can affect the reception.

Celtic View, 18th September 1968

....

Celtic's reserves continued to make fine progress, but not without the odd disappointment. After a 4-2 defeat against Hearts at Parkhead, Sean Fallon accepted that such results were always a possibility, but he was also quick to defend the club's policy of fielding very young teams: *'We could have fielded a more experienced side with players like Cattanach, Gallagher and Murray all looking on but we have decided to blood as many youngsters as possible, and against the stiffest opposition, and that's why we reintroduced Dalglish, Davidson and Wilson.'*

Around this time Kenny missed a few reserve games, and dropped down a level to play Jordanhill College in the combined reserve league. This was a league in which Celtic could field their third team against Scottish lower league clubs and a number of non-league clubs, such as Glasgow Corporation Transport, Glasgow University and Jordanhill Technical College. In one such fixture, Celtic's third eleven beat Jordanhill 5-1. The reason for recalling this game is that Kenny Dalglish scored what is considered to be his first competitive goal for a Celtic team. The Celtic View match report stated that: *'Dalglish, one of the most versatile young players on our staff, was star of the match'.*

Playing in an attacking midfield role, the goals began to flow for the young Kenny. On 23rd November Celtic reserves beat Falkirk in the reserve League Cup semi final, with Kenny scoring a hat trick. The half back line of Dalglish, Connelly and Hay was earning rave reviews, and Kenny was selected to represent the Scottish youth side to face Norway at Cappielow.

This match serves as a splendid example of the high standard of Scottish football at the time, as the young Scots demolished their Norwegian counterparts 8-1. Celtic were represented by Tom Livingstone, Vic Davidson, Paul Wilson and Dalglish. All four boys performed well, with Davidson and Wilson both scoring, and taking the plaudits on the night, along with Rangers' Alfie Conn and Aberdeen's Tommy Craig.

To further illustrate the strength of Scottish football, earlier that day Celtic drew 1-1 against Red Star in Belgrade, qualifying for the quarter finals of the European Cup. The game kicked off at 1.15 pm, and the wonders of modern aviation meant that Celtic could return from Yugoslavia more quickly than when travelling from Aberdeen by train. Dunfermline rounded off a great day for Scottish football, eliminating Greek side, Olympiakos, in the European Cup Winners Cup.

The first setback to Kenny's professional career came in early December, in a game against Hibs at Celtic Park, when he was carried from the field, the victim of bad tackle. Sean Fallon was outraged at the incident, and told the Celtic View: '*We lost Dalglish at the interval with a foot injury. Ken sustained an ugly gash to his instep after contact with an aluminium stud in a tackle and had seven stitches inserted into the wound. I just can't understand why aluminium studs were allowed to be used in this match. I certainly wouldn't allow my players to use them at Parkhead.*'

As the New Year of 1969 dawned, Jock Stein must have been feeling particularly pleased. Celtic sat on top of the league, had won through to the final of the League Cup and, most importantly, had a glamorous European Cup quarter final tie against AC Milan to look forward to. Newspapers talked of another *'grand slam'* of trophies, especially if Stein could negotiate a passage past the Italians. He was also taking a keen interest in his reserve players, and included them in training sessions and practice games as much as possible. He was especially keen to iron out any minor flaws, and Lou Macari recalls Kenny having to practice one surprisingly poor aspect of his game, as he explained to the Evening Times: *'Incredibly, one of the worst aspects of Kenny's game was his finishing. He used to come back in the afternoons and was pushed hard by the management. He practised every day. He'd have a goalkeeper, he'd have a ball at his feet, bang, bang, bang, on and on...'* It was clearly hard work that would prove worthwhile in the years to follow.

After recovering from injury Kenny was included in a Celtic team which travelled to Brunton Park to play Carlisle United in mid January. This game was arranged at the instigation of Jock Stein who was a great friend of Carlisle's manager, Bob Stokoe. Celtic goalkeeper Ronnie Simpson was happy to renew his acquaintance with Stokoe on the night, as both men had played for Newcastle United in the 1955 FA Cup final, when United defeated Manchester City 3-1. Kenny Dalglish wore the number seven shorts that night, although he played in midfield. Sadly, the match was played in torrential rain and had to be abandoned after fifty six minutes, with the score at 1-1, and players from both teams slipping and sliding around in treacherous conditions.

As spring approached, the Celtic v AC Milan European Cup ties were the most anticipated games in Europe. On 19th February, 500 Celtic fans set off from Glasgow on chartered planes to follow their team. However, the official Celtic party were later required to fly from Prestwick because of snow at Glasgow airport. When they arrived in Milan they discovered that the Milanese were suffering from similar harsh weather.

Milan had sold 81,000 tickets, giving them world record gate receipts of 204 million lire. This was approximately £136,000, an extraordinary sum of money in 1969. Italian ticket touts were said to have lost a fortune as many fans stayed at home, after eight inches of snow fell in a five hour period through the night. The famous San Siro had to be covered in plastic sheets and an army of two hundred men worked to clear the snow. Celtic players and officials were pleased to be reunited with German referee Kurt Tschenscher, who was in charge in Lisbon when Celtic won the European Cup. The West German official deemed the game playable after a pitch inspection, although Celtic officials complained that the lines on the field were obliterated by snow.

The game was played with little incident and finished in a 0-0 draw. Milan fans threw fireworks and fire crackers after the game, venting their disappointment with their team. Celtic became favourites to go through in the second leg.

Jock Stein encouraged all his young players to watch Celtic's big European ties at Parkhead for a number of reasons. The most obvious one was to cheer the team on to victory. Another was to learn from watching the continental superstars who paraded their talents. The return leg against Milan was to be no different, with Kenny Dalglish and his team mates looking forward to watching the great Gianni Rivera, the outstanding Italian player on show. Also on display would be their expensive foreign imports, West German defender Karl-Heinz Schnellinger, Swedish winger Kurt Hamrin and Brazilian striker, Angelo Sormani. This was the most keenly anticipated European tie in Scottish football history and the game was an all ticket 75,000 sell out. So great was the demand for tickets, a Glasgow bookmaker reputedly paid an incredible £30 for two fifty shillings stand tickets.

The match was something of an anticlimax, with the only goal coming from Milan's Pietro Prati in the 12th minute. Billy McNeill failed to control the ball from a Jim Craig throw in, allowing the nippy Prati to race in on goal and coolly score. Celtic attacked constantly for the rest of the game, but to no avail, and the Schnellinger inspired Milan defence held out for a 1-0 victory. It was a night of utter frustration for the Celts, while the Milan player danced for joy at the final whistle.

The Italians went on to win the competition, beating Manchester United in the semis and Ajax in the final. Nereo Rocco, Milan's legendary manager, said that he knew his side would win the trophy following their victory at Celtic Park, as Celtic were the only team he feared. Such was the esteem in which Stein's team were held at that time.

A cloud hung over Parkhead after the Milan defeat, but it would soon be blown away by a whirlwind, as Celtic's first team and reserves went on to enjoy a period of tremendous success. The league title was clinched in dramatic fashion on 21st April, when Celtic came back from 2-0 down against Kilmarnock at Rugby Park. They drew 2-2, and a point was enough to give Stein's men their fourth successive league title.

....

An unknown Celtic fan saves Kilmarnock's league flag, Daily Record 23 April 1969

Kilmarnock's 1965 league flag was stolen during the 2-2 draw with Celtic at Rugby Park on Monday night. An anonymous caller phoned the Daily Record to say that the flag was in locker 114 in Queen Street railway station. Two policeman arranged to have a passkey open the box, and found the flag wrapped in brown paper, with a letter on top. The letter was written by Celtic fan, JMcC, who said that the flag had been stolen by three Celtic supporters. JMcC and his mates had followed them outside and found them about to burn the flag. They had then 'confiscated it.' The letter said 'my friends and I thought this was a senseless act, but then the police came and we didn't want to be accused of stealing it.' Kilmarnock manager, Walter McCrae, was at a meeting in Glasgow yesterday and came to collect the flag. Kilmarnock won the title in 1965 and are entitled to fly it at all home games. A man later walked into the Daily Record office at 5.30 last night and handed in key 114. He asked 'Did you get the flag then?' When told it had been returned he said, 'Good, I can go home and have my tea now.'

....

With Kenny Dalglish now well established as the reserve right half, Celtic reached the semi finals of both reserve cup competitions. In the League Cup the Celts lost to Aberdeen in the semi final, which took place over two legs. They had to face Aberdeen once more in the Scottish reserve cup final, again to be played over two legs. The Dons were favourites to win. Like Celtic, Aberdeen had a marvellous reserve side, with quality players such as Jimmy Smith, Tommy Craig, Martin Buchan and Arthur Graham, all of whom would earn lucrative moves to English clubs in due course.

In the first leg at Pittodrie Celtic played tremendously well to win 2-0, with goals from George Connelly and Charlie Gallagher, and Danny McGrain was the star man in opposition to Aberdeen's highly rated teenage left winger, Tommy Craig. In the second leg at Parkhead Celtic again won 2-0, this time with goals from Lou Macari and Vic Davidson. After the match the Celtic players were presented with the trophy and George Connelly was hoisted aloft by his team mates to show the cup off. This was an exciting time for Celtic's budding young players, and for Kenny Dalglish, who was now Celtic's established reserve right half, it was an especially proud occasion, as this was his first winners medal in senior football.

Aberdeen's renowned scout, Bobby Calder, was responsible for securing talented young players for Aberdeen. Calder and Sean

Fallon were involved in an ongoing tussle, competing for the signatures of promising boys. In a Celtic View interview in 1969 Calder recalled his competition with Celtic, stating that: *'Sean Fallon just pipped me for young Kenny Dalglish. Pat Crerand was another of my near misses but to be fair to myself I've more than evened the score since.'*

....

Celtic fan Charles Murray recalls a humorous side to the Old Firm rivalry from the period.

> 'In the late 1960's Colin Stein joined Rangers from Hibs for a Scottish record transfer fee of £100,000. The film, 'The Good, the Bad and the Ugly ' was a popular release around this time. Celtic fans humorously referred to it as, 'Jock Stein, Frankenstein and Colin Stein', although there was much debate amongst the support as to whether the bold Colin was actually the bad one or the ugly one!'

....

Shortly before the second leg of the cup final against Aberdeen, George Connelly was dramatically drafted from the reserves into the Celtic side, to play Rangers in the 1969 Scottish Cup final. Celtic's two established wingers, Jimmy Johnstone and John Hughes, were both out through suspension and injury. Consequently Rangers were seen as huge favourites to win, so much so that a party had been arranged after the game for the Gers to parade the cup. The exit gates at Ibrox were to be opened straight after the final whistle so that Rangers supporters could flood straight in from Hampden for a victory celebration.

However, Jock Stein was to display his tactical prowess for this match. He played Connelly and Bertie Auld as wide men, but instructed them to drop back into midfield in what is thought to have been the first instance of a Celtic team playing a 4-4-2 formation.

The Rangers full backs, expecting to face two orthodox wingers, pushed up the field, leaving Rangers central defensive pairing of John Greig and Ronnie McKinnon totally exposed against the pace of Celtic's strikers, Bobby Lennox and Stevie Chalmers. Celtic took a very early lead, when Billy McNeill was left unmarked and scored from a corner kick. As half time approached Celtic caught Rangers with two killer blows. Firstly Lennox used his great pace to race clear to score, and then came the game's defining moment. At the edge of the Rangers' penalty area John Greig inexplicably lost possession to young Connelly. He proceeded to calmly dribble around Rangers' keeper, Norrie Martin, and place the ball in the net. A most remarkable feat for a young player to show such composure, appearing in his first Scottish Cup tie in front of a vast crowd of 132,000.

At half time the Celtic players were euphoric in their dressing room, a most unusual occurrence in an Old Firm game of any kind, let alone a cup final. Their supporters were in a similar mood for the entire second half, and their joy increased when Chalmers added a fourth after being clear on goal. Bertie Auld said in later years that he had seen this game take place twice, the first time on Stein's tactics board the day before, when the Celtic manager had explained to his players how the game would develop, and then again during the match itself.

In the aftermath, Alex Ferguson, who was Rangers' centre forward that day, took a great deal of flack for failing to prevent McNeill scoring the crucial opening goal, as it was his job to mark the Celtic centre half. He was so disappointed that he threw his loser's medal away and he never played for Rangers again.

....

The Evening Times reports justice being served in a Glasgow court, 28th April 1969

*After being fined £5 at Glasgow Marine Court today, Celtic fan Michael McGhee asked the magistrate - 'Can I have my horn back?' The horn was confiscated by police when McGhee was arrested after the Scottish Cup final on Saturday. McGhee, 22, of 39 Closeburn Street, Possil, admitted a breach of the peace in Keppochill Road. Mr Kevin Breslin, the Fiscal, said McGhee was shouting, 'Celtic are the f****** champions', and, 'we are the people.' He was making a noise with a horn, the type found on motor vehicles. Baillie Thomas McLaren asked McGhee,' Do you want it for next year ?' He then told the court officer, 'Give him his horn back. Judging by Saturday's result it looks as if he will be playing it for some time to come.'*

....

In the space of three weeks in April 1969 Celtic won all three Scottish domestic trophies, another remarkable record that Jock Stein could add to his growing list of achievements. Celtic's domination over Rangers and Scottish football in general was unquestionable.

....

We do not intend to refer again to the records of 'firsts' that Celtic have achieved. But one feat to which we will refer is quite unique. Never before have a Scottish club won all three trophies within a month. This month Celtic have annexed the League Cup, First Division Championship and the Scottish Cup, and because of the extra strain involved, this is a magnificent achievement.

Celtic View editorial 30th April 1969

....

Connelly's cup final appearance was a huge boost for the young Celtic players. This was the first time one of Celtic's youngsters had been selected to play in a major game, and it showed that the Celtic management had faith in fielding their young reserves. What

Connelly had achieved, the others would now aspire to. Sean Fallon showed great satisfaction when he summed up the development of his young charges in the Celtic View at the end of the season: *'As far as the youngsters are concerned their progress over the season has been most encouraging. Remembering that most of these players were only youngsters when we competed in the Italian youth tourney last summer, their progress over the last few months has been remarkable. Although we are delighted that the boys have lifted one of the second eleven trophies, this is not the prime objective of the reserve team. If we had been determined to win prizes I am convinced we could have lifted the reserve championship by fielding our strongest team at all times. However, the main object of the second eleven is to groom youngsters for the top team and this would not be achieved by playing first team pool players instead of youngsters.'*

Kenny Dalglish poster from 1975 which was won in a competition in the Celtic View.

Kenny lines up for Cumbernauld United against Celtic in May 1968. He is second from right on front row.

Celtic's youth team parade a flag before the Montecasale tournament in Italy in May 1968.
Kenny can be seen third from right.

Kenny is on the ball against Raith Rovers on his league debut for Celtic at Parkhead on 4th October 1969.

Happy Celtic players pose for a picture in 1970. From right - George Connelly,
Kenny Dalglish, Vic Davidson, Lou Macari, Davie Hay and Davie Cattanach.

A young Kenny poses for the camera in 1971.

Kenny celebrates scoring against Rangers reserves at Parkhead in April 1971.

Kenny watches Lou Macari fight for possession against Falkirk in the 1971 reserve cup final second leg at Brockville in May 1971.

Kenny scores his first goal for Celtic, a penalty against Rangers at Ibrox, on 14th August 1971.

Kenny scores against Stirling Albion
at Celtic Park on 26th August 1972.

Kenny scores against Ujpest Dozsa at Parkhead in the European Cup on 25th October 1972.

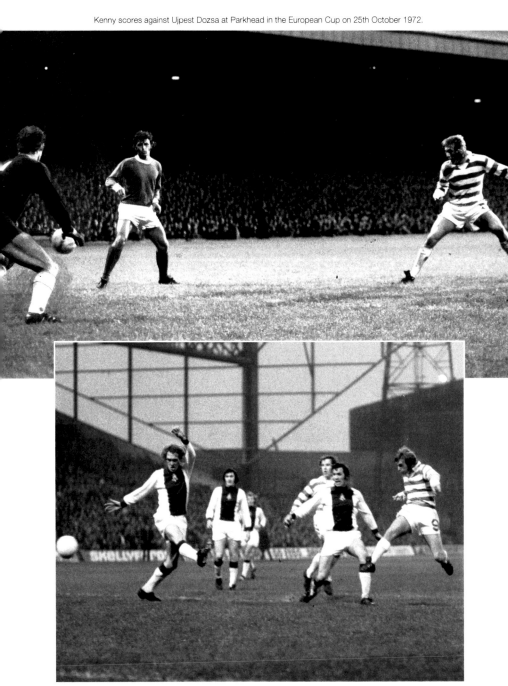

Kenny scores against Hearts at Parkhead on 18th November 1972.

Davie Hay, Billy McNeill, Dixie Deans and Kenny Dalglish celebrate after Dixie opens the scoring at Easter Road on 28th April 1973, on the day Celtic won their eighth consecutive league title.

CHAPTER FOUR
LEARNING FROM THE GREATS · 1969/1970

In the summer of 1969 Kenny travelled to Jersey with a group of friends, including the young Rangers player, Alex Miller. In an issue of Goal magazine from that period, Kenny recalled an amusing holiday incident on the island. *'We were with a crowd of our mates when some English lads challenged us to a Scotland v England match. They put on a big act thinking it was going to be easy but what they didn't know was that most of us were professionals. Just about the only time they touched the ball was when it was centred. We won 20-0 and became popular with the other Scots holidaymakers who cheered us whenever we played.'*

By the start of season 1969-70, Celtic's young players had become the talk of Scottish football. They had already built themselves quite a reputation, and there was great anticipation amongst the Celtic support as to who would be the next boy to make the break through into the first team. This would be no easy task, as competition for places was already fierce, and during the course of the previous season Celtic had purchased midfield man Tommy Callaghan from Dunfermline, and striker Harry Hood from Clyde. Both players commanded considerable fees for the time. Callaghan and Hood were hugely experienced, and had gone straight into the first team squad, making things just a bit more difficult for any reserve player trying to make his mark. It was also an indication that Jock Stein had judged that his young charges were not yet ready and would have to be eased along gently.

In an interview with the Celtic View, given in August 1969, Sean Fallon indicated that it would be no mean feat for any Celtic reserve player to emulate George Connelly's progress to the first team: *'We don't set targets but if we get one or two lads each year who prove themselves equipped for first team duty we feel we are doing exceptionally well. The standard is high - they must be if this club is to continue to be a force in world football - and clearly not everyone measures up. This is the sadder side of football. You become attached to the boys and it's a wrench when you have to part with some of them. But our function is to provide players of a top calibre for the first team. The aim is to ensure that every position is adequately covered. It's not good enough to be a reserve. A youngster must have his ambition to have a place in the first team pool. And incidentally we don't think or talk about players at Parkhead as reserves. We look on all of them as Celtic players.'*

It would clearly be a difficult process for the young Celts, and sacrifices had to be made as Lou Macari later told the Evening Times: *'We had no social life. If you took your girlfriend out to a restaurant on a Saturday night, that was a big deal. We wouldn't dare be seen in a pub, never mind a club.'* The financial and professional rewards in football were great for those who were successful, and Jock Stein's guidance had to be followed as Lou knew well: *'It went to the extreme of not drinking Coca-Cola. Jock would go mad if you did, he thought it wasn't good for you. The players had to be in bed by ten before a match. He even told you what to eat, you didn't get a choice.'*

If following Stein's principles could be hard for young men to adhere to, the bonus came with training under the great man himself. Stein worked hard and expected his players to do likewise, and he spent a great deal of time and energy polishing the rough edges of his young charges, as Kenny Dalglish would later recall, when speaking in the Celtic View: *'Jock liked to know all about his young players and he spent lots of time working with the reserves. Once he told me off for playing square balls which could be intercepted by opponents. I listened and I understood but I repeated the mistake until he pulled me aside and told me to play sweeper. All the time he was watching and correcting little points with the other lads, managing to keep us all on our toes.'*

The young Celts were expected to be versatile. Players were required to adapt to play in a variety of positions in reserve games, and the days of playing in a particular position were over. Danny McGrain came to Celtic as a half back, but would later settle into his full back role, and would go on to be regarded as world class in that position. Even Kenny Dalglish was occasionally required to play as a defender, not because he had particular potential to play there, but to get a better appreciation of different positions and to help improve his way of thinking on the field of play.

The reserves first game of the new season was against Airdrie at Broomfield, with Celtic running out winners by 5-1. Long time Celtic fan George Murray recalled this game as the first time he had taken notice of one particular young Celt in action: *'I first saw Kenny Dalglish at Airdrie in a game at the start of the season. For some reason Jinky had been left out of the big team and because he was playing for the reserves we went out to Broomfield, my Dad, my brother and I. There was a red faced youngster playing right half for the reserves and my reaction to him was just as it was when I first saw Lubo Moravcik - this guy can play. It wasn't that he did anything spectacular, just the grace with which he received the ball, moved it on and glided about the pitch. He was never hurried and you could tell he was a talent. A few months later Bobby Murdoch was injured and Kenny was picked to play at right half. I said to my pal when the teams were announced - 'this boy is some player' and he fitted in seamlessly to the big team. He always seemed to have a red face and his smile when he scored was something to behold - I often think of him when I watch these ludicrous celebrations these days.'*

Four days later the reserves played Rangers at home in a sectional League Cup tie. Celtic thrashed their city rivals 5-0, with two goals apiece from Vic Davidson and Lou Macari, and one from Jim Brogan. Rangers had a few experienced players in their side, which made the result all the more impressive. One week later the young Celts travelled to Ibrox to record a 1-0 win. Vic Davidson scored the winning goal in a game in which Rangers' goalkeeper, Norrie Martin, saved his team from a thrashing similar to that of the week before. Even Jock Stein was moved to comment to the press on the performances of his boys. He had some encouraging words, stating that: *'Some of these youngsters will be knocking on the first team door in the not too distant future.'*

Reward for this fine start to the season was soon to come Kenny's way. Celtic had been drawn against Basle in the European Cup, and Stein named Dalglish and Danny McGrain in the Celtic party to travel to Switzerland for the first leg. They were not there to be considered for selection, but to sample the experience of travelling abroad and the atmosphere of being in a foreign stadium. This was both exciting and educational for the two young Celts, and Stein would continue with this policy of taking a couple of reserve players on each trip abroad. Celtic returned from the St Jakob stadium with a respectable 0-0 draw, and won the second leg 2-0.

The Swiss air had obviously done Kenny no harm. On 20th September, a few days after he returned home, Celtic reserves again thumped their Rangers counterparts, in a league game, this time by a margin of 4-1. Kenny was required to play in a defensive role as sweeper, an unusual position for him. Sean Fallon was delighted with the outcome: *'Teamwork, tenacity and brilliant individualism were key points in our victory. Young Ken Dalglish has recently been playing a free running style of football. Here we changed his role to play it tight with centre half Cattanach. Dalglish adapted admirably and was one of the reasons Ronnie Simpson had so little to do.'*

On the same day as the reserve victory, the Celtic first team won 1-0 at Ibrox in their own league fixture. This was a notable result, as they played the last 25 minutes with only ten men, after Jim Craig was ordered off after an altercation with Willie Johnston. Rangers had brought Jim Baxter back to Ibrox during the close season, and the hope was that Baxter would inspire the Ibrox men to the form of their previous glory days. As it was, Baxter had no influence on the game, and he looked short of fitness. The experiment did not work, and within a few months *'Slim Jim'* retired, having become disillusioned with the game.

....

Bobby Murdoch explains the difficulties of watching Celtic, rather than playing for them, as Celtic win at Ibrox.

> *'When I am a spectator it is sheer misery. Only when we get two or three goals in front can I relax. I just can't bear to watch Celtic against Rangers. Every time the ball goes anywhere near our goal I am biting my nails. Rather than watch our league game at Ibrox I went to Perth to see St Johnstone play Aberdeen. And even then with fifteen minutes left I came out and sat in the car listening to the game at Ibrox on the radio. It was just as agonising as spectating, but when the whistle went and we won I was on top of the world.'*

Celtic View, September 1969

....

Young Kenny Dalglish continued to make headlines with the Celtic reserves. However the Celtic youngsters blotted their copybook when they suffered their first defeat of the season. They were beaten 3-1 by Dundee in a league Cup tie played at Celtic Park. Two weeks later the Celts travelled to Dens Park for the second leg, hoping to redeem themselves. They dredged up every ounce of energy they had to win 5-1 after extra time, going through 6-4 on aggregate. Sean Fallon was glowing in his praise for their display: *'This was the best performance of the season...Dalglish was outstanding.'*

On the morning of Saturday 4th October Celtic fans opened their newspapers and were greeted with two stories regarding their team. Firstly, Celtic had drawn Benfica in the European Cup, a much anticipated but difficult glamour tie, with the great Eusebio destined for Glasgow. Secondly, a young man named Kenny Dalglish was pictured smiling. Jock Stein had named the Celtic side to face Raith Rovers at Parkhead and Kenny was listed at no 4. He was set to make his league debut, in place of the injured Bobby Murdoch.

Stein had informed Kenny on the Friday that he was to play. Kenny was then able notify his father, who watched him play in every game, not to attend the reserve fixture but to come to Celtic Park instead. Bobby Murdoch made a point of visiting Kenny in the dressing room before the game to lend him some encouragement. He had to point out to his young colleague that he was trying to put his boots on the wrong feet! Dalglish was understandably nervous, and this light hearted incident helped to clear any nerves.

The young Celt had a fine debut, performing admirably as Celtic romped to a 7-1 win, impressing Jock Stein in the process. He stated in the Celtic View: *'Dalglish was not carried away by the first team names. He played an effective role in the victory and gave us authority in midfield. His cross field service to Callaghan and Hughes was quite an eye opener for the fans.'*

The Daily Record was equally complimentary: *'Stein dropped a bombshell on Raith - a kid called Kenny. In his league debut Kenny became the latest of Celtic's instant heroes. The young right half refused to let the first team tempo kill his obvious skill. He used the ball well and wasn't afraid to get involved in the sophisticated soccer of some of his more famous team mates.' All in all, a great start to Kenny's Celtic league career.'*

Four days later Kenny was a surprise choice in the Celtic side to face Ayr United at Hampden, for a League Cup semi final tie.

Despite being favourites, Celtic struggled on the night, and it took a Bertie Auld goal in extra time to save them from defeat, in a 3-3 draw. Dalglish created one of the goals and played well enough to retain his place for the replay, played again at Hampden. Ayr were under the guidance of their new manager, Ally MacLeod, who was to be become one of the big personalities in Scottish football. The Ayrshire men put up another spirited performance, but lost narrowly by 2-1. Dalglish was very impressive in this game, and could have scored twice. He was denied by Ayr goalkeeper, David Stewart and also recorded a narrow miss. With 78 minutes played Ronnie Simpson badly injured his shoulder. He was withdrawn, requiring Tommy Gemmell to go in goal for the last 12 minutes. Gemmell held out and Celtic went through to the final, but sadly Simpson's injury was to end his career.

....

Aston Villa manager Tommy Docherty discusses his support for Celtic.

'I supported Celtic as a boy and always wanted to play for them. Unfortunately I did not play for them as long as I would have liked, but I still have the greatest respect for the club and all the people connected with it. On a Saturday I always look for the results of Celtic, Preston and Chelsea, in that order.'

Daily Record, October 1969

....

Dalglish made an impression in both semi final ties, but he then returned to the reserves to continue his development. On 18th October Celtic were required to call off their league game against Dundee United, in order to keep Gemmell, McNeill, Johnstone, Lennox and Hughes rested. They were all in the Scotland squad for the World Cup qualifier, to be played against West Germany in Hamburg.

The fans' focus turned to the reserve side, and the attendance of 13,000 at Celtic Park was Scotland's largest crowd of the day. The fans were rewarded by a 5-1 victory over Kilmarnock. Kenny Dalglish scored twice and Sean Fallon commented on another change of role for Dalglish : *'Kenny was given a run at centre forward and responded with two goals from the penalty spot. He did quite well in the middle and is gaining positional experience. He is the type of player you can move around and seldom has a bad game.'*

Scotland lost 3-2 to the West Germans in Hamburg, ending their hopes of qualifying for the World Cup, to be staged in Mexico in 1970. Unfortunately, Celtic defender Tommy Gemmell was involved in a controversial incident, in which he was sent off for assaulting the West German forward, Helmut Haller. Three days later Gemmell was left out of the Celtic team to face St Johnstone at Hampden in the League Cup final. Gemmell felt aggrieved at being punished by his club when he had transgressed while playing for his country. He rather justifiably claimed that Stein would not have dropped him had Celtic been playing Rangers in the final, and not the Perth Saints.

Gemmell's misfortune presented an opportunity for young Celtic reserve David Hay, who was promoted to the first eleven to play in his first senior cup final, on 25th October. Hay had been in the side sporadically since the season started, but was not yet regarded as a regular first team player. Celtic beat St Johnstone 1-0 through a Bertie Auld winner, and young David earned his first medal. This was yet another boost to the youngsters at Celtic Park, showing that progress was indeed possible.

....

Celtic are a box office success in the cinema.

The film show of the 4-0 Scottish Cup Final win over Rangers in April, to be shown at the La Scala picture hall in Glasgow on

Sunday 9th November, is now sold out. 1,000 fans will attend, in two screenings. As it has been such a success, the film show will be repeated on 30th November, with all takings being donated to charity.

Celtic View, 4th November 1969

....

A young Celtic side had the pleasure of travelling to Dublin in early November, beating amateur side University College Dublin 10-0. Lou Macari was making a name for himself as a goal scoring striker. He claimed four goals on Irish soil, with Kenny Dalglish getting two, Davie Cattanach two and Billy Murdoch scoring once. The other goal was credited as an own goal by the Dublin side.

On their return from Dublin, Dalglish and Macari were overjoyed to learn they were both to start in Celtic's next first team game, against Hearts at Parkhead. They had been selected as Jock Stein wanted to keep Harry Hood and Willie Wallace fresh for the European tie against Benfica at Celtic Park. However, there was disappointment for Kenny and Lou when Hearts provided the shock of the day, winning 2-0. Hearts goalie, Jim Cruickshank, was in great form, pulling off one particularly stunning save from Dalglish. Although he was to return to his reserve beat, Kenny had been given a taste not only of first team football, but of the big occasion at Hampden, and it no doubt whet his appetite for more of the same.

In the first leg of their European Cup tie against Benfica, Stein turned to his experienced men, and Gemmell, now back in favour, opened the scoring with one of the most spectacular shots ever seen at Celtic Park. Wallace and Hood added two more. John Hughes was frustrated when his goal was disallowed for an infringement. Benfica were troubled by Celtic's pace in attack, and they suffered a blow when Eusebio, who looked unfit, was taken off at half time. Celtic won convincingly in the end by 3-0.

Interestingly, Artur Jorge, who appeared as a substitute for Benfica, was heavily rumoured to have been in contention for the Celtic manager's job in the summer of 1997. However, Wim Jansen was ultimately appointed by Fergus McCann.

....

Celtic fans return to Lisbon on a pilgrimage to support the team against Benfica.

> *Celtic won't be without support at tonight's game in Lisbon. Apart from the hundreds of friends they made on their last trip to Portugal, nearly 1,000 fans will travel to Lisbon. Just under 500 will fly to the game, while hundreds more are travelling by road and rail. Benfica have set aside more than 1,000 tickets for Celtic fans.*

Celtic View, 26th November 1969

....

The second leg in Lisbon proved to be one of the most dramatic games in Celtic's history. The Celts were 2-0 down, deep into injury time, when Diamentino scored with the last kick of the ball. This caused so much confusion that the players were unsure if the referee had blown for time up or awarded a goal. However the delirious Benfica supporters seemed in no doubt. They poured onto the pitch causing Laurens Van Ravens, the Dutch referee, to lead the teams off the field and into the dressing room. Five minutes after the ball hit the net it was announced the scoreline was 3-3, and the game would continue into extra time. Celtic then showed their resolve and defended resolutely until the end of the extra period.

In 1969 European ties which finished level after extra time were decided on the toss of a coin. The normal practice in this situation was for the referee to lead the two captains to the centre circle and toss the coin into the air. This would allow the spectators to see from the triumphant captain's reaction which side had progressed.

Van Ravens appears to have been a bit of a character, and he insisted that the toss be conducted in his dressing room with the two captains, Celtic's Billy McNeill and Mario Coluna of Benfica, their respective managers, two linesmen and a handful of pressmen squeezed into the cramped room. Outside, the club officials packed the corridors of the Estadio da Luz in anticipation. Meanwhile, the fans could only wait and wonder.

Van Ravens asked the Celtic captain to call first. McNeill turned to Stein for advice, only to be told, *'You're on your own.'* McNeill called *'heads'* and won the toss. Van Ravens then informed him this toss had been to determine which of the captains would have the right to spin the coin for the actual decision. He again handed McNeill the Dutch two guilder piece to toss into the air, this time to determine which club would win the tie. McNeill called *'heads'* again. The coin landed on the floor, rolled, hit the referee's foot and lay still. Everyone bent down to have a closer look, and the Celtic captain punched the air in delight when he realised he had made the right call. McNeill was allowed to keep the coin, reported to be worth six shillings in pre-decimal Britain, as a souvenir.

As the Celtic players and officials celebrated in the bowels of the stadium, an announcement was made in Portuguese beginning with *'Benfica'*. This resulted in a huge roar from the home crowd as they thought their team had won. What the announcer was actually about to say was, *'Benfica have lost'*, but in the confusion Celtic fans stood desolate, thinking Benfica had gone through. Many were only informed later by Scottish journalists that it was the Celts who had in fact prevailed.

It was 12.30am, in the early hours of Thursday morning, before the result was finally decided. It proved to be an emotionally draining experience for Celtic fans, players and management. On their return to Glasgow rumours spread across the city that the coin used by the Dutch referee had King Billy's head on it. Actually it bore an image of Queen Juliana, head of the House of Orange.

Kenny Dalglish's fine displays in the Celtic first team had not gone unnoticed, leading to Scotland manager, Bobby Brown, selecting him for Scotland's under 23 squad. The Scots played France at Hampden on 3rd December. Scotland turned on an impressive performance, running out 4-0 winners on the night. John O'Hare of Derby and Peter Lorimer of Leeds both scored a brace. Unfortunately for Kenny he was named as a substitute, alongside Peter Marinello (Hibs), Dave Clunie (Hearts) and David Stewart (Ayr United), and he did not get to play.

However, the under 23's result was to be overshadowed in the media, as Willie Waddell was named as the new Rangers manager. Davie White had suffered a poor start to the season, and was sacked after a humiliating home defeat by Gornik Zabrze of Poland in the European Cup Winners Cup. The Scottish newspaper reporters therefore speculated on another new era at Ibrox.

In contrast to the reserve side who had barely lost a game, the Celtic first team suffered a slow start in their league campaign. This allowed Hibs and Dundee United to enjoy spells at the top of the Scottish league throughout the autumn months. It was not until 17th December that Celtic made it to the top of the table, following a scintillating 7-2 home win against Dundee United. Jimmy Johnstone turned in a performance on that dark winter's night which is regarded by many as his greatest ever.

The Glasgow Herald described Jinky in glowing terms: 'Little Jimmy Johnstone stood tallest. Impossibly he beat three men, four, five. Then, in case anybody had not believed it the first time, he did it again. He flitted past opponents to the inside and outside; over and under; sometimes it seemed he went through them.'

In a fine display of sportsmanship, several Dundee United

players waited at the pitch side to applaud Jimmy from the field, including former Rangers player Davie Wilson, who warmly shook the wee man's hand. Such was Celtic's display that the United manager, Jerry Kerr, exclaimed: *'You do not mind losing to the world's greatest team.'*

....

Celtic players become TV stars as they win the BBC show, Quizball. They beat Sunderland, West Bromwich Albion and Hearts along the way.

> *It was an eventful weekend for Celtic full back Jim Craig. On Friday he was the star of Celtic's win over Hearts in the final of TV's Quizball. On Saturday he put through his own goal to give Rangers a lead. But since the game came right in the end the fans should forgive him this lapse and remember instead his sparkling television performance. Answering difficult questions under the bright lights is not easy, but Jim did it magnificently. He was ably supported by Billy McNeill, Willie Wallace and celebrity supporter, John Cairney.*

Celtic View, 25th February 1970

....

In the next round of the European Cup Celtic were drawn against the Italian champions, Fiorentina, with games scheduled for March 1970.

....

The Celtic View reports on the team's home based Italian supporters.

> *Whatever happens tonight, Celtic fans will be able to see their team in action, as a live transmission of the second half will be shown on BBC1 starting at 10.05pm. But even that is not enough for some supporters, as they will be going to Florence for the*

game. Among them will be the Casa d'Italia, an Italian club from Park Circus, Glasgow. Many of the members come from the Lucca province, near Florence. But that won't count tonight, as the Casa d'Italia are going to Florence to root for Celtic.

Celtic View, 18th March 1970

Both the first team and the reserve side continued their excellent progress in the early months of 1970. Lou Macari became a regular first team squad player, but disappointingly for Kenny Dalglish, he was not to appear in the senior side again until the end of the season. Celtic recorded memorable wins over Fiorentina in the European Cup, and Rangers in the Scottish Cup, as they continued their relentless pursuit of success. The European Cup semi final draw paired them with Leeds United. This was sensational news, and was the first time Scottish champions and English champions had faced each other in Europe's premier competition.

Leeds were England's strongest side, featuring many international players, and were managed by renowned manger, Don Revie. Revie and Jock Stein were close friends and had attended the Open golf championship together at Royal Lytham in the summer of 1969, won by Britain's Tony Jacklin. Leeds were no strangers to the Celtic fans, having faced Celtic in Glasgow for pre season friendlies in 1968 and 1969. Celtic had failed to win either game. In view of this, Leeds were favourites to go through over two legs, despite Celtic's greater European experience.

Kenny travelled south to watch the first leg at Elland Road, with reserve team mates John Gorman and Davie Cattanach, and Stenhousemuir player, Alex Smith. Smith was a great friend of Leeds' Scottish captain, Billy Bremner, and he had arranged for all four of them to stay at Bremner's house whilst in Leeds. Smith drove the boys south and they were overjoyed to meet

Leeds players Jackie Charlton, Peter Lorimer and Eddie Gray at Bremner's house. John Gorman recalls that the young Celtic boys sat enthralled until four in the morning discussing the football matters of the day. At this time Bremner would have been in fine spirits, as he had just been named as England's Footballer of the Year, a most notable achievement.

There was a bit of gamesmanship before the first game, played at Elland Road. Celtic were informed they could not wear their traditional white socks as Leeds also wore white. Leeds offered them a choice of red or blue socks. For any Celtic team blue was obviously not an option, so the Celts turned out in red socks, causing Jock Stein to comment humorously in the Daily Record: *'Under their floodlights they'll show up more orange than red, and our supporters will think that we're wearing the colours of the Irish tricolour. That'll please them.'*

Celtic brought a large contingent of 13,000 fans to Elland Road, and they were delirious when George Connelly gave them the lead with only 40 seconds played. Celtic, inspired by the midfield duo of Murdoch and Auld, were the better team in the first half. Connelly scored again in the second half, only for the goal to be disallowed for a marginal offside decision.

In the end Celtic won 1-0, and had sixteen shots at goal, compared to six for Leeds. Celtic were so impressive that Bill Shankly commented in the press : *'Every manager in England should have been here tonight for an object lesson on how the game should be played.'* The Scottish press typically went overboard, with Hugh Taylor reporting that: *'It was a victory that should have been accompanied by the pipes of the Scots Guard, a roll of drums and a commentary by Laurence Olivier.'* The entire occasion had been a tremendous public relations coup for Celtic. The club were inundated by letters from publicans and hotel proprietors, as well as members of the Leeds general public, commending the Celtic fans for their good behaviour. On their return to Glasgow's Central station on 2nd April, more than 5,000 Celtic fans thronged the platforms. As the team's train arrived the fans burst into song, and when Stein appeared they chanted his name, echoing it loudly throughout the station.

Stein was quick to remind everyone that this was only half time, and that the second leg would be a difficult hurdle. Four days before the return match, Celtic suffered a real blow, when surprisingly they lost the 1970 Scottish Cup final. They were defeated 3-1 by Aberdeen at Hampden, in front of a crowd of 108,000. The game was a most controversial one, with match official, Bobby Davidson, awarding a series of crucial decisions against Celtic. Stein was said to be livid with Davidson's display. It was clearly not the ideal preparation for such an important European tie.

In view of the massive interest in the match, the Celtic directors chose to move the home game against Leeds to Hampden. Tens of thousands of fans queued outside Celtic Park for days to purchase the highly desired briefs. Some were so desperate that they met Leeds fans at Central station in the hope that they could buy any spare briefs the Leeds fans may have brought north.

A staggering 136,505 spectators crammed into Hampden on 15th April to watch the game. To this day it remains a record attendance for a European tie, and is unlikely ever to be beaten. Billy Bremner, playing a real captain's role, silenced the massive crowd by giving Leeds the lead on the night, with as fine a shot that the old ground had ever witnessed. In the second half Celtic were by far the dominant team, and the fans drove them on with the incessant, deafening chant of *'Celtic....Celtic....Celtic...!'* Jimmy Johnstone was Celtic's match winner. He tore the Leeds left flank to shreds with a typical display of dribbling wizardry, for which the English defenders had no answer. John Hughes equalised with a header, and then Johnstone set Murdoch up to score the winner, as the Glasgow night sky was pierced by a level of noise surely never heard before.

Kenny Dalglish was in the Hampden main stand watching with his Celtic team mates. Many years later he himself was to describe the atmosphere on the night: *'Although I was a Celtic player I was not a first team regular. I was one of a staggering 136,000 people who combined lungs to create the most moving atmosphere I can ever recall. The atmosphere was something that is difficult to describe. You had to be there to know what I mean. Not just noise but a genuine passion and a driving, urgent will for Celtic to win. When Celtic went 2-1 up the crowd erupted with such frightening ferocity that the stand actually began to shake and creak. I really looked up to the ceiling and thought it was going to collapse on top of us. The crowd did not let up and the whole place shook to its foundations, it was unreal.'* Kenny Dalglish Soccer Annual 1979.

It should be pointed out that not every Scotsman inside Hampden that night was a Celtic supporter. The *'Battle of Britain'* tag had united the vast majority of Scots fans behind Celtic, and many neutrals who attended found themselves caught up in the fervour created by the crowd. This was a time when the vast majority of football fans still worked in the traditional heavy industries of shipbuilding, car plants, mining and engineering. When Celtic won at Hampden the voices of the west of Scotland working classes echoed around Europe.

....

Celtic personalities are in demand at Downing Street after reaching the European Cup final.

A Downing Street honour came Celtic's way this week. Jock Stein, Billy McNeill and their wives were invited by the Prime Minister to a reception at number 10. The occasion last night was in honour of the Swedish Prime Minister who is visiting Britain. As ill luck would have it neither Mr Stein or Billy were able to go. With European and domestic competitions now reaching a climax, Mr Stein found his commitments to Celtic made his attendance impossible. Billy's wife recently had a baby and did not yet feel up to taking part in an occasion of this kind. Manager and player regret having to turn down the invitation and the chance of a football chat with the knowledgeable Mr Wilson, who has recently had the happy experience of seeing his team, Huddersfield Town, return to the English first division.

Celtic View, 19th April 1970

....

The Celtic reserves then continued the good example set by the first team. A tremendous season for the Celtic boys was rounded off when they clinched the reserve league and cup double.

The team topped the league, scoring an astonishing 116 goals in the process.

	P	W	D	L	F	A	PTS
1. Celtic Reserves	34	27	4	3	116	36	58
2. Rangers Reserves	34	21	8	5	95	34	50
3. Aberdeen Reserves	34	20	8	6	95	34	48

The reserve cup was won over two legs, by defeating Dunfermline 4-3. This served to round off a magnificent season for the young Celts. Their top goal scorers were Lou Macari (50), Vic Davidson (44), Kenny Dalglish (20) and Jimmy Quinn (20).

Sean Fallon was glowing in his praise of his young *'students'*. He reserved particular praise for Dalglish, commenting that it had been a great achievement for him to score so many goals from the midfield role which he had now made his own.

As a fitting reward the reserve side travelled to Milan on 6th May to watch their more experience colleagues take on Feyenoord in the European Cup final. David Hay and George Connelly had graduated from the second string and were now established first team players. They were now looking forward to taking part in the biggest game in European club football, with millions of people watching live on television.

....

Celtic fans are given a warning on currency exchange valuations before travelling to Milan for the 1970 European Cup final.

If you're going to Milan don't let the large amounts of Lire to go to your head. For there is 1500 Lire for every £1 although this is subject to slight variations. So even a Lire millionaire isn't all that rich. Here's a quick calculation to how your money should go.

£1.....1500 Lire

10s....750 Lire

2s......150 Lire

1s......75 Lire

A thousand Lire bank note is worth 13s 4d.

Celtic View, 29th April 1970

....

By 1970 Dutch football was just coming to prominence, and Feynoord's most notable display en route to the final came when they eliminated the tournament favourites, AC Milan, 2-1 on aggregate.

Celtic were strong favourites to win the game, given that they had won the trophy in 1967, and also had previous experience of playing in the San Siro, against AC Milan in February 1969.

The San Siro had been a controversial choice of venue, having hosted the European Cup final as recently as 1965, when Inter Milan defeated Benfica 1-0, at the Italians home ground. Many observers felt that another country should have the privilege of hosting the event.

As Celtic landed on Italian soil, Archie McPherson recalls how Jock Stein informed him of a face of the future: *'The first time I was aware of Kenny was in Malpensa airport in 1970 when he was helping to carry the Celtic hampers, and Jock confided in me that he believed this boy was going to be a great player. Even on the eve of a European Cup final, Jock was looking forward.'*

The contrast between Lisbon in 1967 and Milan in 1970 was startling. In Lisbon the locals welcomed the Celtic fans with affection. However, in Milan municipal strikes paralysed the city, leading to rumours that the cup final venue would have to be moved to Rome's Olympic stadium. The Italian authorities confirmed that the final would remain in Milan, after an *'11th hour appeal'* from Italy's director of sport and tourism. Both sets of fans endured horrendous transport problems. Malpensa airport struggled to cope with 20,000 Celtic fans arriving from Scotland, and a similar number flying in from Rotterdam. In Lisbon the game was played in late afternoon, on a beautiful sunny day, whereas in Milan the match would take place in the darkness of an evening of unseasonably wet weather. At the match Celtic fans would find themselves split up inside the stadium, situated behind both goals. Their singing would largely be drowned out by the Feyenoord fans' loud hunting horns, causing immense frustration.

Since arriving at Parkhead in 1965, Jock Stein had been almost flawless in his tactical approach. Sadly, on this huge occasion, he was to make a rare mistake. In the two Leeds games Celtic played in a 4-3-3 formation, with a midfield of Murdoch, Auld and Connelly. In Milan Connelly was left on the bench as Celtic reverted to a 4-2-

4 formation, allowing Feyenoord to dominate in midfield, with the advantage of an extra man in their 4-3-3 set up.

It all started so well when Tommy Gemmell gave Celtic the lead, with a trademark powerful shot. However Feyenoord equalised almost immediately afterwards, through Rinus Israel. Celtic goalkeeper, Evan Williams, kept the Celts in the game with a string of fine saves. Tragically, with only 3 minutes remaining in extra time, an unusual error by Billy McNeill allowed Ove Kindvall to score the winning goal. Feyenoord became the first Dutch club to win the European Cup. They were not to be the last.

After the game there were huge delays for return flights to Glasgow. Shocking stories emerged of a total lack of security, with fans actually wandering around on the runways, desperately looking to board a flight back home. Back in Glasgow, public houses had been issued with late licences, allowing them to open until 11.15pm, but the punters sloped off in disappointment after the final whistle, preventing the pubs from making any real profit from the Celtic fans.

Ironically, Feyenoord midfield player, Wim Jansen, was later to become Celtic manager. He arrived in the summer of 1997, at Celtic's time of greatest need. Rangers were the dominant force in Scotland and were going for a record breaking tenth consecutive Scottish league title. Jansen reportedly took the job because of his admiration for the Celtic side of 1970. He brought the great Henrik Larsson to the club, and both men inspired Celtic to a dramatic last day title win in May 1998, dashing Rangers' record breaking aspirations.

....

Alex Ferguson recalls following Celtic to the 1970 European Cup final.

'In 1970 I travelled to Milan to watch Celtic play Feyenoord in the European Cup final, with Ayr manager Ally MacLeod, Partick

Thistle manager Davie McParland and Hibs' manager, Willie McFarlane. I found it an expensive business being a Celtic follower that day. Every restaurant in Milan seemed to be shut. Finally we found a Hungarian eating place that was open. They took us in all right, in more ways than one, for the meal cost us around £8 each. It was a good job the air fare was reasonable.'

Celtic View, 15th January 1975

....

For the first time Jock Stein faced criticism from Celtic supporters and the Scottish media. On their return home Celtic players faced accusations that they were too interested in the financial inducements available to them, and had underestimated Feyenoord in the process.

Stein was forced onto the defensive in the summer edition of the Celtic View, published in June 1970: *'I still feel that our failure in this game was very largely due to the fantastic build up given to our games with Leeds. Let's face it, in the eyes of the football world this was billed as the final before the final. One excuse that has been bandied about is that the players had business interests which interfered with their football but I don't subscribe to this at all. Like all successful teams the players started a scheme to protect themselves from outside interests capitalising on their success. These arrangements were started before the matches with Leeds and they had no adverse affect on the semi final performance. Neither did they interfere with the final.'*

....

Celtic had many famous fans supporting them in Europe. Acclaimed actor, Peter Vaughan, recalls following them to Milan in 1970.

A few eyebrows were raised when it was learned that the principal character in the new ITV drama series 'Fox' was to be called King Billy. But prepare yourselves for a big shock... in real life King Billy is a Celtic supporter. This was revealed by Peter Vaughan, who plays the major role in 'Fox'. When he visited Scotland recently, he admitted that he's Celtic daft. He travelled to Milan in 1970 to see the Parkhead side lose 2-1 to Feyenoord in the European Cup final. 'The first thing I do on a Saturday night is pick up the paper to see how Celtic got on.'

Daily Record 1st March 1980

....

Within days of returning from their disappointment in Milan, Celtic were required to fulfil a prior commitment by going on a North American tour, where they would play games in America, Canada and Bermuda. Jim Brogan, John Hughes and Jimmy Johnstone all stayed at home due to injury, allowing Stein to name Kenny Dalglish, Lou Macari and Vic Davidson as part of the travelling party. This was a series of games that Celtic could well have done without. However, having being greeted by despondency back home, the Celtic party were delighted to receive a noisy welcome from two hundred Canadian Celtic fans on their arrival at Toronto airport.

Just twenty four hours after arriving in Toronto Dalglish and Macari were named in Celtic's starting eleven to face Manchester United. Celtic lost 2-0, in a game in which United disappointed the large crowd by defending and playing on the break, which they did to great effect. It was then on to New York, where the Celts drew 1-1 against the Italians of Bari. Davidson was the only young player on show on this occasion. Celtic then travelled back to Toronto for a 2-2 draw with Bari, a game which was actually abandoned with three minutes remaining. The Italians took exception to Celtic being awarded a penalty and walked off the field of play in protest.

The amount of travelling was taking its toll, and Jock Stein left the tour early to return home to have a troublesome ankle problem looked at. Sean Fallon was left in charge, and unfortunately was required to send Tommy Gemmell and Bertie Auld home from New York, following an alleged misdemeanour at the Irish-American club in Kearney, New Jersey

David Cattanach then joined the Celtic party in Boston to maintain squad numbers. In Boston, Dalglish, Macari and Davidson all played against a local team described as a *'Boston Irish select'*. Celtic won 7-1 and Davidson grabbed the headlines with a hat trick. A tired Celtic team played their final match against Eintracht Frankfurt in New York, where they lost 3-1.

After the trauma of losing to Feyenoord and the arduous schedule of travelling across North America, the exhausted Celtic party were happy to conclude their itinerary with a week on the island of Bermuda. Two games were played against local sides, which would hardly be testing matches, even for the tired Celts. Kenny didn't play in the 7-1 win over a Bermuda select, but appeared in the final match, a 4-1 win over the Somerset cricket club, in which he scored from a penalty.

The Bermuda trip was said to be hugely enjoyable affair, following the stresses and strains of a long season, and one which the young Kenny would remember fondly for many years to come. Kenny described the trip in the Kenny Dalglish Soccer Annual, 1979: *'My most memorable trip came when I was 18 and went on tour with Celtic to Canada, America and Bermuda. I found Bermuda breathtaking. The memory of arriving on that magical, beautiful island is as vivid to me now as it was then. Strangely I found it similar to Jersey in some respects - the size of the island and the slow, almost lazy pace of life is something that they both have in common. The climate though, is totally different. I will never forget tucking into breakfast in bed in the hotel and eating delicious fish and fruit in that romantic paradise when only a short time previously I was getting stripped for matches in wooden huts when I was playing with Glasgow United. Vic Davidson and I hired pedal start mopeds and went riding on roads with 20 miles per hour speed limits.*

The sight of the sea and the sand and seeing film star Dustin Hoffman, who was staying in our hotel, produced wonderful memories of Bermuda.'

Kenny Dalglish must have spent the summer of 1970 heartened that his progress over the course of the season meant he was now considered a member of Celtic's first team squad. The next hurdle would be to establish himself as a regular first team player.

CHAPTER FIVE
BANGING ON THE DOOR - 1970/1971

A pall of disappointment hung over Celtic Park in the summer of 1970. For five years Celtic had been accustomed to a diet of almost constant success. Therefore the fans were disillusioned following the defeat to Feyenoord in Milan. Despite winning the League title and the League Cup, the season was generally regarded as a disappointing one. This was indicative of the high standards Celtic fans had come to expect. However, as the new season approached, Celtic were preparing well to go through the entire process again, and their attitude was typified by their enthusiastic trainer and long time Stein lieutenant, Neilly Mochan: *'Old players are supposed to sit back and polish their medals. I have no time for that, I'm too busy preparing Celtic to win more medals!'*

....

Celtic have a foreign admirer.

Despite what happened in Milan Celtic still command a great deal of respect on the continent. In a recent interview, Rene Hussy, who coaches Swiss side Grasshoppers Zurich, was asked which foreign team he rated highest. He replied: 'For me, Glasgow Celtic are the most complete side playing in Europe.' Hussy was recently appointed as interim coach of the Swiss national team.

Celtic View, 12th August 1970

....

With the first team playing a few pre-season games in Ireland, Celtic reserves started the season by beating Stenhousemuir's first team by 2-0. Kenny Dalglish was injured in the second half, and when he retired to the bench he was surprised to find the famous Scots' actor, John Cairney, sitting there. Cairney was a huge Celtic fan, and when he arrived at Ochilview to watch the match the Celtic officials had beckoned him to the bench. Cairney was well acquainted with the Celtic squad at the time, having been Celtic's celebrity player in the BBC's Quizball TV show, which they had won twice.

After this match Kenny and the second team travelled to Brunton Park, to play against Carlisle United. The game was a replay of the previous friendly between the sides, which had been abandoned due to poor weather conditions in January. The young Celts tore the second division side apart in a 5-2 victory, with Jimmy Quinn scoring a hat trick. Celtic's left back, John Gorman, was so impressive in this game that Carlisle pursued his signature, and he signed shortly after, going on to have a very successful career south of the border.

As the new season dawned, Sean Fallon explained to the Celtic View how the club were developing their young talent: *'The policy regarding the reserves at Celtic Park has always been the same - to rear young players to a degree of skill, fitness and character that they need to become first team material. We like to win but even victory becomes secondary to the all important aim of producing a ready made stream of players for the top team.'*

In August Danny McGrain became the latest graduate from the reserves to move up to the first team. He made his league debut at right back against Morton, and then kept his place for the vital opening Old Firm encounter in September. McGrain was in direct opposition to Rangers' volatile left winger, Willie Johnston, and this was seen as a real challenge for the young Celt. McGrain had a superb match, totally nullifying Johnston. Celtic won 2-0, with a convincing display, and could even afford the luxury of a missed penalty. Bobby Murdoch scored one of the finest goals ever seen at Celtic Park, when Jimmy Johnstone dummied the ball at the edge of the area, allowing Murdoch to run on to it, sending a thunderous shot into the net. It was struck with such ferocity that it was said the noise of the thudding ball could be heard in the press box. Stein was so delighted with McGrain's performance that he waited at the side of the pitch at full time to salute his player personally.

Rangers' manager Willie Waddell suggested before the clash that Celtic were not the team they had been in previous years, but the Celts proved him wrong on the day. Celtic fans seized on this and chanted the following, aimed at Waddell, to the tune of the popular TV show, *'Dad's Army'*:

Who do you think you are kidding Willie Waddell
When you say the Celts are done
We are the Bhoys who will stop your little game
We are the Bhoys who will fly the flag again
So who do you think you are kidding Willie Waddell
When you say the Celts are done!

....

Letter to Celtic View, 16th September 1970.

We read in the press Rangers are to follow the example of the Commonwealth Games athletes by building up for big games on 'Nutrament.' This has been described as liquid food and we are told Tommy Craig, the Rangers trainer, has been given samples to see if the club will adopt this as a pre-match meal. But we know there is nothing to beat the Jock Stein food - 'Winalot.'

....

In the first round of the European Cup, Celtic were drawn against the Finnish champions, Kokkola. In the first leg Celtic won 9-0, with young winger, Paul Wilson, scoring twice as the latest recruit from the reserves *'conveyor belt'* of talent. Celtic were nine up with 20 minutes left, and at one point it looked as if they might record the biggest win in their history. However they appeared to take pity on the bedraggled Finns, and the Celtic fans gave their opponents a sporting ovation at the end.

Kenny Dalglish was included in the squad for the second leg, when Celtic travelled to Kokkola, a town only 150 miles south of the Arctic circle. This was the furthest north a European Cup tie had ever been played and the unfortunate Jimmy Johnstone took ill on the five hour flight. He had to be laid across three seats for the journey. This would have been extremely difficult for him, as Jimmy had a well documented dislike of flying, and he subsequently had to spend the entire duration of his time in Finland in bed.

On their arrival in Finland, Jock Stein was asked to organise a *'spectacular'* training session to take place before the game, as so many of the locals wanted to see them play. The Celtic party found the weather bitterly cold, but the people of Kokkola were very welcoming, and before the match a quaint announcement was made over the loudspeaker: *'We hope the lesson you are about to give us will be to our benefit in future'*. Dalglish replaced Bobby Murdoch in the second half as Celtic ran out winners by 5-0, and a massive 14-0 on aggregate.

....

Celtic receive a unique honour, Celtic View 1970.

Celtic are already certain of at least one trophy this season - from the France Football newspaper. A representative of the club will fly to Paris in September to collect it. It's a replica of the famous statue, Victory of Samothrace, which stands in the Louvre in Paris. It has been rewarded to Celtic for last season's performance in Europe. In the previous two seasons they were runners-up.

....

In the domestic game the Celtic reserves continued to progress, not only winning games, but playing attacking football and scoring a multitude of goals. Jock Stein liked to pit the skills of his reserve side against senior sides in the Scottish second division, and John Fallon recalled one occasion when the young Kenny was to realise that there was more to learn about being a Celtic player than simply playing the game: *'One night we played East Stirling in a friendly match and there was a boy from East Stirling who Kenny was running riot against. The boy had a go at Kenny and called him a 'Fenian B******' which was quite upsetting. Five minutes later Davie Cattanach went right through him and told him - 'That's how a Fenian B****** tackles!'*

Perhaps Kenny remembered this incident when he gave an interview to the Celtic View a short time afterwards: *'Sometimes what players say is just as bad as their tackles, that really makes you want to flare up but it would only be a victory for folk who say these things if I did.'* The self discipline he displayed in those formative years was to serve him well throughout his career.

Even by their own high standards, the Celtic reserve side were having a exceptional season. But, by the end of 1970, frustration began to kick in, with some of the boys becoming disheartened at their lack of first team opportunities. Since the start of the season Kenny had made only two appearances as substitute in the first team, and having experienced the big time atmosphere in the previous campaign, there was concern that he might not make the breakthrough to first team regular.

Andy Lynch had been a team mate of Kenny and Vic Davidson at Glasgow United, and he recalls the frustration of both young Celts at that time: *'I had broken through into the Hearts first team and occasionally Kenny, Vic and I would play snooker in the afternoons after training. They were a bit envious that I was playing regularly for Hearts and said that they thought they thought they would have to consider leaving Celtic in order to get first team football elsewhere. I told them they were mad to even consider it and they were playing for one of the best clubs in Europe and that they should stick it out.'*

Unknown to Kenny, his talents were being coveted by others around that period. Andrew MacLeod, son of the late Ally MacLeod, tells the interesting tale of his father pursuing Dalglish while he was manager at Ayr United: *'Around 1970 Ally approached Celtic to see if Kenny Dalglish was available for transfer. He had been impressive against Ayr in the 1969 League Cup semi final games, and Ally had kept an eye on him after that. He was told by Jock Stein that the reserve players were Sean Fallon's responsibility, so he spoke with Sean who said that he wanted to give Kenny a bit longer to make the breakthrough. Ally used to say that Kenny would have been an Ayr player if it wasn't for Sean's faith in him.'*

As 1971 dawned it was clear that this would be a vital year in Kenny Dalglish's career. However, the year was to start on a tragic note for Scottish football. On 2nd January, Rangers hosted Celtic at Ibrox in the traditional New Year fixture. The game was played on a misty afternoon, and was fairly uneventful until Jimmy Johnstone gave Celtic the lead in the 89th minute. Tragedy then unfolded after Colin Stein equalised . Some Rangers fans had started to exit the stadium at stairway 13 in the traditional Rangers end. There was an accidental surge forward down the stairway, which tragically resulted in sixty six people losing their lives. The emergency services tried in vain to save lives at the side of the pitch, as Rangers and Celtic officials attempted to aid them. Kenny watched the game from the Celtic end terracing, and would undoubtedly have been badly affected by this tragedy. It would have been highly likely that he would have had family and friends in the Rangers end of the ground, where as a young boy he would have stood to watch matches with his father. In later life Kenny would sadly have to endure similar tragedies, in 1985 at Heysel and in 1989 at Hillsborough.

In March there was bitter disappointment at Parkhead, when Celtic lost 3-1 on aggregate to a Johan Cruyff inspired Ajax side, in the European Cup quarter finals. With their European adventures over for another season, the league title race was also proving to be a struggle for Celtic.

Aberdeen had gone on a marvellous run of fifteen consecutive league victories between October and January. Their goalkeeper, Bobby Clark, created a record, going 1,155 minutes without conceding a goal. This was a record that would last until 2014, when it was surpassed by Celtic goalkeeper Fraser Forster. At the beginning of April Aberdeen led Celtic by four points, but significantly Celtic had three games in hand. The title race was desperately close, and would be decided on 17th April when Celtic travelled to Pittodrie.

Before then Celtic had to negotiate their passage to the Scottish Cup final, by playing underdogs Airdrie at Hampden. The Diamonds shocked everyone by coming back from 3-1 down to grab a 3-3 draw. Jock Stein kept his team selection for the replay under wraps until near kick off, and there was a great deal of surprise when Kenny Dalglish was named at inside left, in preference to his close pal, Vic Davidson. This was his first start in the Celtic senior side since November 1969, and he seized his opportunity. Kenny put on an impressive display, creating Celtic's goals in a 2-0 win.

....

He made such an impression that he was the subject of much media publicity afterwards, as this Daily Record interview showed:

Celtic starlet Kenny Dalglish admitted shyly yesterday that he is one of the luckiest players in Scottish football. For the 20 year old who has played just five matches for the Parkhead first team, has made three of those appearances at Hampden - the ground on which every player hopes to play one day. Says Dalglish: 'Here I am just beginning the game and already I have played three times at Hampden and yet there must be many players who have gone through a whole career hoping to play there and never made it.' Dalglish, just 20, retains a youthful wonder that all this is happening to him. He still retains a youthful shyness. But there is no evidence of either characteristic in his play. He admitted he was nervous before the start of the game against Airdrie on Wednesday night. He said: 'I didn't find out that I was playing until an hour before the match. I can get nervous before the start of a reserve match, but on Wednesday I seemed to be all right even kicking around at the start. Then I seemed to tighten up. I made a couple of bad passes to start with then I put in a good tackle and began to feel better. After that I was happy with my play and thought I did all right.' He did. In fact the way he calmly stroked the ball about in midfield made it difficult to believe that he came to Parkhead as a striker. Kenny explained: 'When I joined Celtic I was sent to Cumbernauld who were playing their first season in the juniors. I won a statuette for finishing as top scorer with about 30 goals. But it was decided at Parkhead that I was too slow for a striker.' That decision has paid off for Dalglish - and Celtic - in midfield. Dalglish made the first team at the beginning of last season. Then he played against Ayr United in the League Cup semi final and the replay too. Last Wednesday he played in another replay and now he is back in the reckoning. But Kenny says sensibly, that he can't expect to play in the first team every week. With typical shyness he added: ' Of course it would be great to be in the first team every week. But with the amount of good players at Parkhead I realise that I will have to step down some time.' But the boy with the Hampden flair will be back as a midfield ace. There is nothing more certain.

....

Kenny kept his place for the next match, a disappointing 1-1 home draw with Dundee United, which put even more pressure on the Celts for the trip north to face Aberdeen.

In early 1971 rumours circulated that Jock Stein was to leave Celtic, to take over from the ageing Matt Busby at Manchester United. Unknown to the public, Stein had been approached, and he had considered the offer for some time, before declining United's approach. He had chosen to inform his players of his decision before the match against Aberdeen, hoping this would act as ideal motivation for them before such a big game. A win for Aberdeen would all but give them the league, and Celtic knew they had to avoid defeat to retain any chance of keeping their title. Over 15,000 Celtic fans travelled north to lend their support, and with Stein turning to his experienced players for such a vital game, Dalglish returned to reserve duty. Celtic scored first through Harry Hood, but when Aberdeen equalised they put the Celts under real pressure. The major incident in the match took place in the second half, when Arthur Graham burst through on the Celtic goal. Evan Williams just managed to touch the ball, and as Graham swept round the keeper, Williams caused the Aberdeen man to hesitate fractionally, before shooting at the empty goal. Inspirational captain Billy McNeill made the save of the match, by recovering to block the shot on the goal line. From that moment on the title belonged to Celtic.

The next few weeks were to be the turning point in Kenny Dalglish's career. On 22nd April Celtic reserves clinched the reserve league in style, when they thrashed their Rangers counterparts 7-1 at Parkhead. Celtic had fielded Bobby Murdoch in an attempt to get him fit for the Scottish Cup final. As Murdoch was playing in his normal right half position, Kenny was required to play further upfield in attack, and he had a sensational game, scoring four goals in his new role as a striker. Fate can be a funny thing. Had Murdoch not played, then there's every chance Dalglish would have continued to play in midfield, and would not have had the opportunity of playing as a striker. He reprised his role in the forward line on 26th April, when the reserve side again beat Rangers convincingly, this time by 4-1, in the reserve League Cup final first leg. Kenny scored one of these goals, with Lou Macari, Ward White, and Vic Davidson claiming the others.

The games were coming thick and fast, and on 24th April Celtic reserves beat Falkirk 4-0 in the reserve cup final, first leg. Kenny and Ward White shared the goals with a brace apiece. Twenty four hours later Celtic's senior side played Ayr United at Hampden. They required just one point to clinch their sixth consecutive league championship. The game was moved from Celtic Park to the national stadium, due to construction work taking place on Celtic's new main stand.

As reward for his fine form Kenny was given a place on the bench, and he replaced Willie Wallace with 15 minutes left, in a 2-0 victory. Kenny and the rest of the Celtic players took the salute of the fans at the final whistle, giving the young Celt a flavour of what success was like at the highest level, a feeling he would soon be getting used to.

The following night it was back to reserve duty, as Celtic travelled to Ibrox for the second leg of the reserve cup final, holding a 4-1 lead. The young Rangers side were given their third thrashing in the space of eight days, as Celtic ran out 6-1 winners, with a hat trick from Kenny. On a beautiful spring evening a large Celtic support had turned out at their rivals' home ground in expectation of another big Celtic win, and they were not disappointed. They taunted the Rangers support by singing 'we want seven!', and the Rangers fans disappeared into the night long before the end.

Life in the forward line was clearly agreeing with Dalglish, and as well as becoming a great goal scorer, he was also a scorer of great goals. George Murray recalls a memorable Kenny goal at Ibrox from that 6-1 romp: *'As I recall it - and you have to remember it was over 40 years ago - Davie Cattanach dispossessed a Rangers forward and passed it out right to Danny McGrain. Danny advanced and Lou Macari peeled off to the right wing and Danny passed it up the line to him. He drew a Rangers defender and crossed it - Kenny met it on the run and hit it on volley from the edge of the box and smashed it into the net past Gerry Neef. Several years later I saw him get a similar chance for Scotland and he pulled it down to control it - probably what an experienced pro would do - but that night he played without fear and simply battered it. Four touches and it went from our box into their net. Rangers had a very strong team out that night as they had been thrashed in the two previous games - I think that players like Colin Jackson and Derek Johnstone played. There were really big crowds and the backing they got, especially at Ibrox, was brilliant. Some of the best football I watched was played by the reserves. In those days they really were a class above everything else in the Scottish game.'*

Even at reserve level, the three wins against Rangers were impressive results. The aggregate score was an astonishing 17-3 for Celtic, with Dalglish claiming eight of those goals. What is also remarkable was that Kenny played three games on consecutive evenings, for a combination of first and second teams. This is in stark contrast to the highly rewarded players of the millennium, who often claim to be jaded after playing just two games in a week. It is testament to the fitness of Celtic's young players that they could not only play so many games in a short period, but turn in impressive, winning displays in the process.

Sean Fallon was delighted with his young charges and gave them this glowing tribute in the Celtic View: *'The entire team were great and I know they won't mind if I select for a special mention the inside trio of Davidson, Macari and Dalglish. They were magnificent. Their displays brought back memories of some older fans of the fine pre-*

war trio of MacDonald, Crum and Divers. Kenny Dalglish has been outstanding. Apart from his shooting ability he has created many chances for his colleagues.'

The reserves rounded off the season on 5th May, when they beat Falkirk 2-1 in the reserve cup final, second leg. They won the trophy 6-1 on aggregate, in a season where they won all three reserve competitions. The league was won as shown:

	P	W	D	L	F	A	PTS
Celtic Reserves	34	23	7	4	108	51	53
Hearts Reserves	34	23	5	6	94	46	51
Kilmarnock Reserves	34	20	7	7	80	46	47

In the process of winning the three cups open to them, they scored 150 goals in total, Davidson (40), Dalglish (23) and Macari (18). The team were truly living up to the 'Quality Street Gang' nickname bestowed on them.

On 8th May Celtic and Rangers drew 1-1 in the Scottish Cup final, in front of 120,092 spectators. Jock Stein was annoyed that Celtic lost a late goal, having being in control of the game. Four days later the replay attracted a crowd of 103,332 and Stein made one vital change, with young Lou Macari replacing Willie Wallace in the Celtic attack. This was another master stroke by Stein, as Macari gave Celtic an early lead. Harry Hood later scored a penalty to make it 2-0. Although Rangers pulled a goal back in the second half, the game belonged to Jimmy Johnstone. *'Jinky'* gave a typically brilliant display of dribbling, which demoralised his opponents long before the end.

In the Celtic end of Hampden the fans waved *'inflatable Jinkys'*, small blow up figures of a wee red haired man in a no 7 Celtic strip, in tribute to their hero. This final is widely considered to have been one of Johnstone's finest games. Newspapers reported that the wee man was so hyped up after the game he played music until three in the morning. He then went out and walked his dog as he was still so full of adrenalin from the final.

Photographs from the time show the Celtic celebrations, with Kenny Dalglish and Danny McGrain, now established Celtic squad players, enjoying the revelry to the full.

Forty eight hours after their cup final success, Celtic travelled to Kilmarnock to play in Frank Beattie's testimonial match at Rugby Park. Beattie was a hugely respected player in Scottish football, and he had given a tremendous eighteen years service to the Ayrshire club. He was considered to be most deserving of this lucrative benefit match. Celtic were missing a few members of the first team, who were on to Home International duties with Scotland, so Kenny Dalglish found himself fielded at centre forward. He was now well settled in his attacking role, and scored an incredible six goals in this game.

Most Celtic fans of the period recall this as the game when Kenny finally made his mark, and subsequently became an established first team player. Nevertheless, not everyone was exactly aware of who he was at the time. Scottish media personality, Jim Delahunt, recalls witnessing Kenny's scoring feat with some confusion: *'In 1971 my Dad took me to Frank Beattie's testimonial which was the first football game he'd ever taken me to. I was nine and we were from Saltcoats and Rugby Park was only fifteen minutes away. We had a programme and this young lad was banging in goal after goal and we just made an assumption it was a young guy called Vic Davidson. It wasn't until the next day, when we got the Daily Express delivered, that we discovered it was Kenny Dalglish, or Ken Dalglish as he was sometimes referred to at that time, who had banged in an incredible six goals.'*

After this match Celtic players and officials were delighted to fly out to Israel to play a friendly game, enjoying a well earned sunshine break after a long, hard season. Kenny kept his place in the team when Celtic played an Israeli International select in the Ramat Gan stadium, in front of a 35,000 strong crowd. Harry Hood scored the only goal of the game. There was a lot of sightseeing for many of the party, some of whom were devout Catholics, keen to visit the sights of the Holy Land.

Kenny was said to have turned down the opportunity of visiting Jerusalem's famous wailing wall, remarking, *'If you've seen one wall, you've seen them all'*, giving an example of the wry sense of humour that he was to become famous for in the years ahead.

There would be no more reserve team football for 20 year old Kenny Dalglish. The late positional change to striker had given him a new dimension as a player, and the years of hard work in training were now paying off. The apprenticeship was over and Kenny was about to show the football world that he was now the master of his craft.

CHAPTER SIX
BREAKTHROUGH - 1971/72

Kenny Dalglish's professional career was clearly on the ascendancy, but his personal life was also to see a major change. After morning training sessions the Celtic reserves used to lunch at the Beechwood restaurant, near Hampden Park on Glasgow's south side. It was a favourite haunt of Jock Stein and Sean Fallon. The Beechwood was where Kenny first met Marina Harkins, daughter of the proprietor, Pat Harkins. Celtic fan Tony Griffin recalls an early occasion when Kenny and Marina were seen together as a couple: *'I used to work at the National Savings Bank at Cowglen beside Kenny's girlfriend, Marina Harkins. Marina was a very attractive girl with a bubbly personality, and naturally all the young guys were falling over themselves to get near her. Every time someone chanced his arm and asked her out, they were politely refused. We all assumed she was spoken for, and this was confirmed - and how - when she rolled up for one dance function on the arm of King Kenny! Open mouthed stares all around! Kenny was shy, friendly, and completely unaffected by his growing fame. He often dropped Marina off at the bank after lunch in his little Fiat, and would always chat with the boys.'*

As part of their pre-season preparation Celtic travelled to Ireland to play against Cork Hibernian and Limerick. Jock Stein named a squad of sixteen players, and it included five *'Quality Street Gang'* players who were now firmly established first team members - Hay, Connelly, Davidson, Macari and Dalglish. The season ahead was already being described by many observers as one of transition, as Stein would be required to balance changes in his team whilst keeping Celtic on the trail of winning trophies.

Kenny remained on the bench for the first game against Cork Hibs, but was in the side to face Limerick. This game was put back twenty four hours due to Limerick's GAA hurling final against Tipperary. When the game went ahead, Celtic were awarded three penalties. When Tommy Gemmell missed the first, penalty duties were passed to Dalglish. He scored twice from the spot. He also scored two from open play, bringing his total to four, in Celtic's 6-1 win.

Sadly, in the hours after this match, Celtic legend Charlie Tully died in his sleep. He was only 47 and Celtic officials travelled north to Belfast to attend his funeral. Manager Jock Stein and captain Billy McNeill were pall bearers, with the Falls Road coming to a standstill, as people gathered to pay their respects to the legendary ex-Celt.

Sponsorship was beginning to emerge in the world of football, and the Drybrough Cup was a novel curtain raiser for the new season. Drybrough brewers put up £10,000 in prize money for a knockout competition, to involve the eight top goal scoring teams from the first and second divisions, based on performances from the previous season.

Celtic were paired against Dumbarton in the first game, winning 5-2, with Dalglish scoring four. The Celts then defeated St Johnstone 4-2 in the semi final, with Dalglish scoring another three. This meant that in four successive first team games Kenny had netted 6, 4, 4 and 3. This was a sensational run of form, bearing more resemblance to a golfer's scorecard, than a goal scoring statistic.

The only negative for Celtic came when it emerged that American agents were keen to line up a game between Celtic and Pele's

Santos, in New York's Yankee stadium. However the SFA refused Celtic permission to play as they were involved in the Drybrough Cup. In the final, played at Pittodrie, Aberdeen beat Celtic 2-1.

....

Celtic's English based supporters gather to mark the start of the new season.

More than 600 supporters from all over England will attend a dance on Saturday night in Corby Civic Centre. The dance - organised by the Corby CSC - has attracted people from clubs as far apart as Birmingham, Luton, Oxford, Tamworth and Langley Mill in Nottinghamshire. First prize in the draw to be held on the evening is a trip to Copenhagen for Celtic's European Cup game. Unfortunately, because the dance is on a Saturday, none of the players can attend.

Celtic View, 25th August 1971

....

Kenny was making the headlines with his scoring exploits, and the newspapers were desperate to find out more about Celtic's new star player. A Daily Express interview from early August 1971 paints a picture of a very modest, unassuming and grounded young man: *Young Kenny Dalglish still stares at the camera as if he were having another passport picture taken. And he will reel off - acknowledging anyone's right to ask - the colour of his hair (fairish auburn) the colour of his eyes (blue) and his height (5 foot 9 inches). When it comes to distinguishing features he declares: 'Well they say I'm a bit like Bobby Murdoch.' Which may be confusing unless you know that Kenny is reckoned to be the footballing discovery of the coming season. At 20 he is hailed as Celtic's goal scoring wonder after four years of very careful grooming. He has seen quite a lot of the football world. His grooming has taken him to the Americas, Italy, Switzerland and Israel. 'But these days', he says with a frown, 'you can't go running about getting big headed because you've been in the first team a few times and the sports writers write you up. I've waited a long time to get playing with the big boys in this business. And the longer you are in the game the more you learn things that would never occur to you unless you mixed with the top players and the people who train you.' Earlier outside Parkhead the players finished training and padded anonymously in their every day clothes into their cars - or in Kenny's case, a friend's car - manager Jock Stein told me: 'Don't write too much about him that he feels he has got to live up to it.' It's all part of the grooming. Jock Stein and the club singled out Kenny Dalglish and several other youngsters in 1968 as soccer potential. There was to be no hurrying with such commodities. It is this long term patience that marks the great clubs and it is rubbing off on the youngsters. 'We are not really told how to conduct ourselves but you know within yourself that you would be daft to spoil things,' says Ken. 'It's just like being an apprentice joiner, which I was by the way. You have to wait until you become a journeyman.' Kenny lives at home with his mother and father in Ashmore Road, Merrylee, Glasgow. He was off to meet a girlfriend but he wasn't going to talk about her. His room at the back of his house has the usual souvenir football posters, a photograph or two and lots of replica trophies. 'All right, I have scored a lot of goals recently but you know it's doesn't matter who scores them as long as it's the team. People forget that no one is more important than the team. How good would I be if the others didn't help me?'*

The season was to start in earnest on 14th August, with Celtic due to host Rangers in the League Cup. It would be the first game in a four team section, which also included Morton and Ayr United. The new main stand was being built at Celtic Park, and work was behind schedule, meaning it would not be ready until the end of August. Hampden was also unavailable. Celtic's proposal that both League Cup ties against Rangers be played at Ibrox was eventually accepted by the Scottish League.

Celtic may have been disadvantaged through losing their home status, but Jock Stein put on a confident front beforehand. Once more he refrained from naming his side until shortly before kick off, and when the team was announced Dalglish was named as Celtic's no 9. Despite his recent scoring spree, there was still an element of surprise when Kenny was named in the team. This was Kenny's opportunity to really stake a claim for a regular first team place, and he was to grab it with both hands.

Rangers had recorded impressive pre-season wins against Everton and Spurs, and were full of confidence. Their captain John Greig boasted to the press before the match that, *'Celtic will face the best prepared Rangers team ever.'*

The game was fairly even until the second half, when Celtic went up the gears, and in a 10 minute period it was reported that Celtic could have scored five times. After 67 minutes Jimmy Johnstone lashed home the opening goal. Rangers were still reeling, when Hughes was hauled down in the area for a penalty kick. Celtic's usual penalty takers were Tommy Gemmell and Harry Hood. Neither was playing, so the responsibility of taking this one fell on Kenny Dalglish's young shoulders. Kenny initially glanced at Billy McNeill, who beckoned him to take the kick.

The penalty was to be taken at the Celtic end, and following the huge roar when the award was given, an apprehensive hush came over the fans. As Kenny approached the penalty spot, he bent down to tie his laces and, after composing himself, he placed a firm shot past Peter McCloy in the Rangers' goal. A new star was born, and Celtic players and fans celebrated joyfully. In the end the feeling was that Rangers had got off lightly with a 2-0 defeat, so comprehensive was the Celtic display. After the match it was reported that Kenny's Dad was delighted with the outcome, despite his Rangers allegiances.

Following the match the plaudits poured in for the young Celt. In the Celtic View John McPhail reported: *'Taking that penalty would have been a nerve racking experience for the most experienced player, but*

Kenny might have been playing a practice match so cool was he as he stroked the ball home.'

Hugh MacDonald recalls the penalty from a Celtic supporters' perspective: *'We were shocked he was taking it as he was the new guy in the team, but we realised if he's taking it then Stein and McNeill must have faith in him. In a way it was uplifting as it was a very emphatic finish and - goodness gracious - this young guy just drilled it in. I spoke with him in later years and he said Billy McNeill had handed him the ball and said, 'you take it'. He was very matter of fact about it.'*

Hugh also commented on seeing something that was to become a familiar sight in years to come: *'One of the things I always remember was the way Kenny would celebrate scoring goals. That bright smile, the pink cheeks always flushed with effort, running away and the arms held aloft and chest puffed out after he'd scored. A picture of joy which we all shared in. That was something he always had.'*

Journalist Hugh Keevins also had good cause to remember the day, although he was not at the match: *'The irony is that Kenny scored the penalty on the day I was married. My family were big Celtic supporters and wouldn't come into the chapel until they knew the half time score and then they couldn't wait to get out to find the full time result. After that penalty Kenny was the guy everyone was talking about afterwards.'*

There is no doubt that Kenny showed a lot of courage in taking a penalty in front of a bellowing crowd of 72,000, as his team mate Danny McGrain remarked: *'To do that in an Old Firm match. Well, I've seen seasoned players want to duck out of it.'*

Jock Stein's tactics during the game flummoxed the Rangers players. Jimmy Johnstone played in a roving role away from his usual right wing berth, and he alternated with Dalglish in the centre of the attack. In these early appearances Kenny normally played in the no 9 position, but sometimes dropped deep and played behind the striker, making it difficult for opposing defenders to mark him. Johnstone was recognised as man of the match, but he paid tribute to Dalglish's contribution: *'Being in the middle I knew I could go forward knowing Kenny Dalglish would drop back to cover.'*

The media made a great deal about Kenny's Rangers background as a boy, and there is no doubt that Rangers must have been embarrassed at having missed out on his talents. Kenny himself was later to recall the events of his first Rangers v Celtic game, in the Archie McPherson book, 'The Blue and the Green': *'People used to ask me how I felt playing against the team I had supported as a boy. Nothing. That's how I felt. I had never let the Rangers-Celtic aggro ever affect me, even when I was a boy. I was a professional player playing for a club with a big support and that's what went through my head. I remember the first time I played against them. It was at Ibrox and we were awarded a penalty. I didn't expect to be taking it considering it was my Old Firm debut but Billy McNeill came up to me and asked me to take the kick. I was a bit surprised but it didn't bother me too much. Just when I was about to run up I noticed my lace had come undone so I bent down and slowly and carefully tied it back in place. I know a lot of people must have thought I was suffering a great strain, but I wasn't. I just stood up and scored. I took these games in my stride, which is why I thought we had the beating of Rangers that day. We always beat Rangers for pace up front and so we liked to draw them upfield a bit then hit them with quick balls.'*

Kenny was a revelation within Scottish football and was making banner headlines in the press following his exploits against Rangers. Hugh MacDonald points out that Kenny may have looked youthful but he was very much the finished article: *'By 1971 Kenny was fully formed and ready to come into the team. In later years when the likes of Tommy Burns and Charlie Nicholas broke through they looked frail in comparison, almost like ball boys, but Kenny was strong even at that young age.'*

It is most interesting to reflect that two great players scored their first competitive goals in the top level of senior football on 14th August 1971. One was Kenny Dalglish at Ibrox. The other was Kevin Keegan, who scored his first goal as a Liverpool player, in a 3-1 victory over Nottingham Forest at Anfield. Both players were born within weeks of each other, and in later years it would be fascinating to observe how their careers would cross many times as players and as managers.

One aspect of Kenny's new found success made him uncomfortable. This was being spotted in public. As someone who was now making waves on the field and headlines in the media, his days of relative anonymity were coming to an end. Marina Harkins' work colleague, Tony Griffin, recalls hearing of how things were to change for Kenny: *'On the evening of the 2-0 win over Rangers at Ibrox when Kenny scored the penalty in his first Old Firm game, he had arranged to meet Marina on an early date at the Boots Corner at the junction of Renfield Street and Argyle Street in Glasgow. When Marina casually mentioned this arrangement to her dad as she was getting ready to go, he nearly blew a gasket. Quickly, he bundled Marina into his car and they raced off to the rendezvous. There was Kenny, anxiously waiting for Marina. The car screeched to a halt, and Mr Harkins urgently motioned Kenny to get in, before telling him that his days of anonymity were over. He could no longer stand and wait at any of Glasgow's favoured meeting spots like Boots' corner, under the clock at Central Station, or any such public place.'*

Celtic won their next two League Cup fixtures against Morton and Ayr, but they lost their following match, in a shock 1-0 home defeat to Morton. Celtic were awarded a penalty at 0-0, but this time Kenny blotted his copy book, slicing his shot past the post. This result gave Rangers renewed hope for their second League Cup game against Celtic, to be played at Ibrox on 28th August.

The Rangers game was again goalless at half time, and in a similar vein to the first match, Celtic ran riot in the second half. Kenny scored an opening goal of stunning simplicity. The move started with an Evan Williams throw, from which Bobby Murdoch flighted a glorious pass through the middle to the on running Dalglish. He let the ball drop before crashing a great shot into the net. Tommy Callaghan then scored the goal of the game, with a terrific volley, and Bobby Lennox rounded off the rout with a third goal, for a 3-0 win. Jock Stein had a confident air after the game, when he spoke to the Sunday Mail: *'We didn't score until early in the second half but at the interval we knew we were going to win. The way we were playing we just knew the goals had to come. Our pattern stayed the same and our players just couldn't get on the park quick enough. We knew we would win easily.'*

There was good reason for Stein's brashness, as so many of his players were on top form, from the sublime Bobby Murdoch, to the creative George Connelly, described as being, *'a director of strategy, accomplished in everything he does.'*

Jean Prouff, manager of French side Rennes, who were due to play Rangers in the European Cup Winners Cup, was so entranced by Celtic's performance he was prompted to predict that they would be Europe's outstanding team for the season.

A gala night was held at Parkhead on 1st September when South American champions, Nacional of Uruguay, visited to play in a game to mark the opening of Celtic's new main stand. Celtic President, Sir Robert Kelly, was seriously ill at this time and Jock Stein visited him after Celtic's games to keep him updated. On this occasion Stein proudly informed Kelly that a 60,000 crowd had turned out, and that the new stand was a complete sell out on the night. This delighted Kelly, who told Stein that he remembered the last stand being built in 1928, but it had not sold out completely until 1938. Kelly would also have been heartened to hear of Celtic's emphatic 3-0 win on the night. Sir Robert sadly passed away a few weeks later. Celtic would be seen as much the poorer for his loss, which would have a major impact for many years to come.

The first Old Firm league game of the season was on 11th September at Ibrox, Celtic's third visit within a four week period. Rangers were desperate to make amends for their two League Cup defeats. This time the Ibrox side were to put up a better fight. They led 2-1 at half time, but in the second half Kenny equalised with a low shot on the turn. The game looked like ending in a draw until the last minute, when Macari and Dalglish combined, with Kenny sending a lob to the back post. Incredibly, Jimmy Johnstone, the smallest man on the park, out jumped Rangers defenders to send a looping header into the net for the winning goal. The Celtic fans were ecstatic.

Meanwhile, at Parkhead in the reserve fixture, Harry Hood scored Celtic's fourth goal against Rangers, in a 4-1 win. This goal came at exactly the same time as Johnstone's Ibrox winner. As the fans with radios at Parkhead cheered the news of Jinky's goal, other spectators were unaware that Celtic had won at Ibrox, as they noisily celebrated Hood's goal. Consequently many left the ground believing Celtic had drawn at Ibrox.

The three wins at Ibrox were to become part of Celtic folklore, with Kenny having scored in all three matches. He had made his mark against his boyhood heroes, and in a radio interview for Talksport in 2012 he recalled: *'I used to go to Ibrox with my Dad and we watched all the games, reserve matches, everything. But when you go and play against them, by the way, you get some satisfaction when you beat them after you've been rejected.'*

Kenny had made a great impression in a very short time, in a team which was already full of star players. Hugh MacDonald recalls: *'Celtic fans were not likely to be overawed by any player coming through. We were used to watching the likes of Murdoch and Johnstone and were unlikely to be overwhelmed by any new player. But there was a feeling with Dalglish that we've got a real one here.'*

These were Celtic's Camelot days. On the domestic scene they had won six successive league titles, and had just demoralised their greatest rivals with three wins at Ibrox. They had established a tremendous reputation in Europe, playing the finest sides on the continent, regularly reaching the latter stages of its premier competition. The Celtic reserve side were in a class of their own, providing a steady stream of talented young players to the first eleven. In Jock Stein they had one of the finest managers in Europe, a man coveted by many of the major English clubs.

Off the pitch the impressive new main stand had been completed. It was said to be the finest in Britain, with a unique press box, which seemingly hung in the air. Celtic Park was roofed on all four sides of the ground, offering more spectator cover than any other British football stadium, with the exception of Wembley. A brilliant new floodlight system had been installed, improving lighting by fifty percent. In 1971 Celtic were clearly seen as a modern, progressive club. Rangers, in comparison, appeared to be suffering from an inferiority complex.

....

The British Steel Corporation at Corby - they provided the main beam for the new main stand - are sending the work's band to play at Celtic Park. But the musical entertainment will not be from a steel band or a brass band but believe it or not from a full blown pipe band. The bandsmen will entertain the crowd before the European game with 1903 Copenhagen at Celtic Park.

Celtic View, 15th September 1971

....

In Europe Celtic stuttered against the Danish champions, Copenhagen 1903, losing 2-1 in Denmark, before winning 3-0 at Parkhead. The Copenhagen goalkeeper was Birger Jensen, who would later cross Kenny's path in 1978, when Liverpool beat

Bruges in the European Cup final at Wembley. That night Kenny famously scored the winning goal by delicately lifting the ball over Jensen from a tight angle, which was perhaps his career highlight.

By October 1971 Dalglish's reputation was becoming widespread. Ian Ross was a Liverpool player, and a childhood friend of Kenny. Ross recalls watching the BBC's 'Football Focus', presented by Sam Leitch, in a London hotel before a Liverpool game in the capital. Footage was shown of some of Kenny's goals for Celtic, and Bill Shankly commented to Ross that Dalglish looked a fine player. Ross informed Shankly that Liverpool previously had him at Anfield on trial. Shankly was said to have been furious at the thought of Liverpool missing out on such a talent.

Celtic had a fortunate draw in the next round of the European Cup, when they faced Sliema Wanderers from Malta. They won the first leg comfortably by 5-0, in a mismatch of a game, during which goalkeeper Evan Williams was reported to have had only four goal kicks. Three days later, on 23rd October, Celtic faced Partick Thistle in the League Cup final at Hampden. Newly promoted Thistle were huge underdogs and Celtic fans were expecting a result similar to that achieved against Sliema.

However, things were to go badly wrong for Celtic. Before the game came the disappointing news that Billy McNeill would miss the game through injury. Bobby Murdoch captained the team but McNeill's absence was to be badly felt. The Celtic defence looked unsure from the start, and Thistle sensed that Celtic had been weakened. Incredibly, Thistle raced into a 4-0 lead at half time. When Jimmy Johnstone was taken off through injury after a harsh Ronnie Glavin challenge, it became obvious that this was not to be Celtic's day.

To their credit Celtic battered away at the Jags' defence in the second half. Kenny Dalglish had several good efforts at goal, but young Thistle goalkeeper, Alan Rough, defied him at every turn.

Kenny eventually scored a consolation goal but Thistle ran out deserved winners by 4-1, in what was probably the biggest cup final shock in the history of the League Cup.

Perhaps the ease of the win against Sliema three days previously had lulled Celtic into a false sense of security, but Thistle richly deserved their win on the day. This game was a huge disappointment for Kenny as he was deprived of winning his first medal at senior level.

Celtic were still bruised from their shock cup final defeat when they travelled to Malta for the second leg against Sliema. New signing, Dixie Deans, had arrived from Motherwell, and was taken on the trip to become acquainted with his new team mates. Jock Stein decided to make the trip to Malta something of a break for the players, and the Celtic party flew out early to enjoy some winter sunshine. There was terrific news for Kenny as he relaxed by the pool, when Jock Stein announced that he had been named in the Scotland squad for the game against Belgium. This was remarkable progress for a player who had only been a Celtic regular for three months, and it served to emphasise the impact he had made in such a short time.

There were no floodlights in the Ta' Qali stadium in Sliema, and the Celtic party were amused when Maltese officials boldly brought kick off forward by forty five minutes, to allow for the possibility of extra time!

Sliema actually scored in the first minute, but Celtic came back to win by 2-1. Celtic players later complained that the Sliema pitch was the worst they had ever played on, saying that the pitch was bereft of grass. However this didn't win them any sympathy from their fans, who pointed out that most of the players had been raised playing on Glasgow's infamous red ash pitches, so should have been more than used to such conditions.

....

Celtic receive a warm welcome in Malta.

Celtic fans who travelled to Malta for the European Cup game were made to feel right at home. Which isn't surprising as most of the islanders are 'Celtic daft.' Outside of the island's local sides, Celtic have the biggest following, with Manchester United also big favourites. One party of Celtic fans were guests of the Sliema Wanderers supporters club before the match and said that pride of place in the trophy room was given to the silver salver and pennant presented by Celtic. On the night before the game, Maltese TV screened a Celtic documentary produced and narrated by Celtic fan, Laurence Mizzi.

The Celtic players were delighted when the Maltese players threw their bouquets of flowers into the crowd before the start of their European tie in Sliema. The players would have been somewhat embarrassed had they been the recipients.

Celtic View, 10th November 1971

....

Aberdeen were proving to be Celtic's main league title rivals for a second successive season. When the Dons visited Parkhead on 6th November they were top of the table with a one point lead over the Celts. A magnificent crowd of 64,000 attended, which was 1,000 more than the attendance at England's match of the day, when Manchester City met Manchester United at Maine Road. Kenny showed his versatility once more when he was required to move back to the right half position, and had a fine match. Celtic looked to have the game won, but a freak McNeill own goal late in the game gave Aberdeen a share of the points.

Four days later Scotland faced Belgium in a European Championship tie at Pittodrie. The venue had been chosen to give Scottish fans in the north of the country a chance to see the national side in action. Tommy Docherty had been named as temporary Scotland manager, and had boasted that at International level only Brazil had better talent than Scotland.

Kenny was named as a substitute, and looked on in admiration as Jimmy Johnstone gave his finest performance in a Scotland jersey. Johnstone was often given a difficult time by a section of the Hampden crowd at Scotland games, but at Pittodrie he responded to the tremendous encouragement the crowd in Aberdeen gave him. Scotland won 1-0 through a John O'Hare goal, and Kenny was delighted to make his first International appearance when he replaced Alex Cropley. He clearly made an impression, as the media reported: *'The young Celt is not content merely to pass a ball and stand but to chase it after it is lost.'*

....

Partick Thistle chairman Tom Reid praises Celtic fans in the match programme for their game against Celtic on 27th November. Celtic won 5-1.

> *'This visit gives us an opportunity to thank the Celtic supporters for their wonderful sporting display at Hampden Park after the League Cup final. They stayed on to applaud our lads after the game, and as we travelled back to Firhill by bus. It was a fine example of sportsmanship.'*

....

Kenny kept up a rich vein of form until the turn of the year, with the 5-1 victory against Motherwell at Fir Park on 18th December being a particular highlight. He scored two magnificent goals, one a delightful flick over the goalkeeper and the other a goal which has long remained in the memory of Hugh MacDonald: *'There was a goal against Motherwell which sticks in my memory when he dropped deep, and demanded the ball from goalkeeper Evan Williams. He ran forward and played a couple of one-two's up the park, beat a defender, then lashed a shot past the Motherwell 'keeper. He made it look so effortless, it was like watching a primary seven playing against primary three.'*

Scoring goals like that ensured Kenny continued to grab the headlines, even in a team which had such major talents as Johnstone, Deans, Macari and Connelly. At the turn of the year the Evening Times had no hesitation in naming Kenny as their Player of the Year for 1971, which seemed incredible, given that he'd only been a first team regular since August. Such was the impression he had made in such a short period of time.

If Kenny was popular with the media, he had also become a firm favourite with the supporters. It was not only the denizens of *'The Jungle'* who had taken Kenny to their hearts, he had also built up a large following of female admirers, who no doubt admired his boyish good looks as much as his talent on the football pitch. This was an era when pop stars like David Cassidy and Donny Osmond were becoming poster boys for young girls, and Kenny was by far the most popular player in the Celtic team in this respect.

Theresa Coyle made the newspapers by coming to Celtic games wearing a green and white jersey with a huge heart emblazoned on it, which read, *'I love Kenny'*. She also wore denims with Kenny's name written all over them. The Celtic View reported: *'Theresa Coyle thinks all the Celtic players are great - but one is greater than the others. In fact you could say she has Kenny Dalglish on her heart. And the young Celt is in some pretty distinguished company. Before Kenny arrived on the scene, Cliff Richard was the tops for Theresa, aged 18, a typist from Glenburn in Paisley. But now she finds Kenny's forays into Europe more exciting than Cliff's song for Europe.'*

In late December the Daily Record ran a full page article on the young Celt, at a time when it was most unusual to concentrate on one player. Again, the young Kenny came across as modest and well mannered: *Kenny Dalglish will be 21 in a few months. He has already come of age as a footballer. For Dalglish, so long tipped as the young man most likely to succeed, has succeeded. The latest witnesses to the success which has arrived with stunning suddenness are the players and fans of Motherwell who watched and admired his two superb goals at Fir Park on Saturday. Billy Ritchie was the unfortunate goalkeeper who Kenny made to suffer. But yesterday Ritchie was still talking enthusiastically about Dalglish. 'He's worth talking about, isn't he? I first saw him about two years ago and ever since then I have been sure he would be a great player.'Yet Dalglish doesn't fit the image of a soccer star. He doesn't have the extrovert look and expensive pad of a George Best...or the flash car of a Rodney Marsh...or the outspoken opinions of a Derek Dougan. Dalglish, dressed smartly, has short hair and lives with his parents on the south side of Glasgow and came by bus to meet me. It is obvious that he is unlikely to be spoiled by success. 'Last season I was playing with the reserves and today here I am in the first team having played for my country, which must be one of the greatest honours any player can receive.' It was fitting that Dalglish should score Celtic's 50th league goal of the season on Saturday, for he more than any other is the symbol of the new Celtic. His goals have come just as freely from midfield as the more orthodox striking role. 'I was never a great scorer for the reserves', he says. 'A lot of my goals came from the penalty spot. I enjoy scoring but the most important thing is that Celtic win.' In a season of success there have been one or two disappointments. He says, 'I have played in two cup finals against Aberdeen and Partick Thistle and we lost both.' It is Dalglish's aim to put that right.*

Around this time Kenny reverted to playing in a midfield role, as Bobby Murdoch was out of the side through injury. He was in midfield for the traditional New Year fixture against Rangers at Celtic Park, a game in which the 70,000 crowd were to witness a most dramatic ending. The last attack of the match saw Harry Hood cross a ball into the middle, where Jim Brogan stole in to neatly head home the winning goal. Brogan, a left back, was a most unlikely hero and had taken a gamble in leaving his defensive beat in order to score. The goal came so late that Jim's father had sadly missed it, as he left just before the end of play. This defeat was another hammer blow to Rangers, for whom a draw would have been akin to a victory.

....

Letter to Daily Record, 7th January 1972

'Willie Waddell is right to say that there is a jinx over his team when they play Celtic. The jinx's name is Jock Stein and he can jinx Rangers any time he likes because he's the greatest manager in the game.'

....

An unusual honour came Kenny's way when he was chosen to represent Scotland under 23's, in a game against the West German Olympic team at Hampden in January. The West Germans were keen to play in preparation for the summer Olympics, and they included Bayern Munich's Uli Hoeness in their starting line up. Scotland won 1-0, courtesy of a goal by Willie Donachie of Manchester City.

In the early 1970's The Celtic View ran a weekly promotion called *'Celtic boy'*, where a school age youngster was invited to Parkhead for the chance to meet his favourite player. Jimmy Johnstone had long been the favourite for the majority of young supporters. However he was about to be usurped in the popularity stakes by Kenny.

Neil Logan describes his experience of being a *'Celtic Boy'*: *'I have a personal story which I think highlights the difference in mentality of Kenny to those who think they are superstars just because they pull on a football jersey. In January 1972 Celtic played Clyde at Shawfield and I was picked to be the Celtic View's 'Celtic boy'. A photographer took my photo and asked me to name my favourite player. I immediately said 'Kenny Dalglish', who had arrived in the team that season, scoring goals against Rangers and almost everyone else. I was ten at the time and he was my hero. At that time the process was you got your picture in the Celtic View, and you were then invited to Celtic Park to meet your favourite player and get a photo with him too. A couple of weeks later I turned up around 1.30 before the game against Hibs along with another wee boy to meet our favourite players. He had chosen Harry Hood. Harry came out was all smiles and was friendly with us both and asked who had picked him. The other guy said he had. He asked me who I had chosen and I replied 'Kenny'. Harry then said, 'Come on, we will go and get him', and led us into the dressing room and shouted over at Kenny, 'this wee man is here to see you!' I was of course star struck with the whole team in there. Kenny walked over and asked, 'Did you really pick me as your favourite player?' I said, 'Aye'. He then said, 'You don't have a very good taste in players do you son!' He was genuinely so modest.'*

On 31st January 1972 Kenny had a vitally important role to fulfil, which for once was not on a football pitch. He was best man for his Celtic team mate, Danny McGrain, when Danny and Laraine Dunabie were married at Blawarthill parish church in Scotstoun. Kenny was said to be more nervous about his best man duties than he ever was as a football player. Unfortunately for the happy couple, the lights fused inside the church, with Kenny having to go and find a torch in order for the ceremony to proceed.

Celtic were drawn against the Hungarian champions, Ujpest Dozsa, in the European Cup and Jock Stein was keen to arrange a challenge match against continental opposition to help Celtic prepare. On 7th February the Russian side, Dynamo Kiev, arrived in Glasgow to provide the stern test that Stein had been looking for. On the night it was Kenny who was the best player, scoring the only goal and being, *'magnificently creative'*. The goal was one of the best he ever scored for Celtic. As the Russian defence waited for his pass, when he was still forty yards from goal, he surprised them by breaking through the middle. He clipped a short pass to Macari, took the return in his stride and struck a great shot which gave the Kiev goalkeeper no chance.

Although Kenny had already appeared for the full Scottish side, he was again picked for the under 23's, to play in the prestigious international between Scotland and England. The game was to be played at Derby County's Baseball Ground in February. He was joined by his Celtic team mates George Connelly and Lou Macari, and they faced an England side with very talented individuals, such as Alan Hudson, Tony Currie, Kevin Keegan, Mike Channon and Malcolm MacDonald.

The Scottish press corps gleefully reported on a terrific performance from the Scots' boys, who came away with a credible 2-2 draw on Derby's infamous quagmire pitch. Kenny scored Scotland's two goals and it was reported that, *'Undoubtedly the number one attacker was Dalglish, not a youngster of the future any more but a glittering star of today.'*

George Connelly marked the vaunted Malcolm MacDonald out of the game, and observers commented on his style as being comparable to the great Franz Beckenbauer. A host of British managers had attended the match. One particular player was singled out, amongst all the fine talent on show. Bill Shankly stated in the Evening Times that, *'There was only one player on the pitch and that was Dalglish. Christ, what a player.'*

Tommy Docherty now boasted about the young talent at his disposal, and vowed that Scotland would make the 1974 World Cup finals, to be played in West Germany. Like Shankly, he had been impressed by Dalglish's performance and in his Daily Record column he paid the following tribute to his rising star: *'Only this week I was speaking to some managers down south and I told them that if I was a manager with quarter of a million pounds to spend then I'd try to spend that cash on Kenny Dalglish from Celtic. I rate young Kenny a better buy at that money than Alan Ball. Ball is a good player but I'd rather have Dalglish. Kenny reminds me a great deal of John White but he scores goals as well. Every time I am with Kenny I am left with the impression that the worst day of the week for him is Sunday because he can't play or train with Celtic.'*

Dundee came to Parkhead on Scottish Cup business at the end of February, and were destroyed in a 4-0 defeat, as Celtic looked to be coming into form at the right time. Kenny scored another tremendous goal when he intercepted a bad pass, ran forward, rounded the goalkeeper and calmly placed the ball into the net, earning him further tributes from the media: *'This young maestro is surely the hottest property in football today.'*

Celtic's trip to Hungary to face Ujpest Dozsa on 8th March 1972 was to prove to be one of the most memorable they had enjoyed on their European travels so far - on and off the park. Travelling to the communist Eastern Bloc was notoriously difficult in the 1970's, but 136 hardy souls travelled by chartered flight to stay in Budapest's Duna Intercontinental hotel. Gerry McNee was a budding journalist with the Daily Express, and was sent to cover the tie for his newspaper. In his book, *'And You'll Never Walk Alone'*, published in 1972, he recorded his experience of meeting a very famous couple.

McNee discovered by chance that Richard Burton and Elizabeth Taylor were in the presidential suite on the top floor, as Burton was in Budapest to film the movie, Bluebeard, co-starring Raquel Welch. Sensing a possible scoop, he went to the top floor and, surprised at the lack of security, found he was able to speak to Burton without difficulty.

Burton was intrigued to hear McNee's stories about working class Celtic fans who were paying an exorbitant £9 per night to stay in the hotel. McNee offered him tickets for the Celtic game, but Burton had to decline due to filming commitments. Both men spoke for a while and Burton impressed McNee with his knowledge of Scottish football, even asking if it was true that Rangers would not sign Catholic players. He also told McNee that he'd watched Celtic win the European Cup in 1967 live on television. Burton was impressed by the fanaticism of the travelling Celts and informed McNee that he would organise a party for them in his suite at his expense. He also invited the Celtic party, who sadly had to decline, as they were travelling back to Glasgow immediately after the match in order to prepare for their important league match against Aberdeen.

Burton gave McNee a hand written letter to pass to Jock Stein. It read: *'Dear Mr Stein, would you he good enough to extend our good luck and best wishes to you and your men for tonight's clash. We will be shouting ourselves hoarse even if only catching glimpses on television. Since Elizabeth is half Scots by blood and one of my brothers married a Scotswoman, it means that I have four Scots nephews and nieces. So again, good luck, RB and ET.'*

McNee found himself in the difficult situation of persuading the Celtic fans in the hotel that Richard Burton and Elizabeth Taylor *really did* want to meet with them, whilst at the same time keeping it from the other reporters to preserve his exclusive story.

A raging storm took place just before kick off, which almost resulted in the match being postponed, with lightning flashing across the Budapest skyline. The tie was shown live by STV, giving them the highest viewing figures of any television programme in Scotland for that week. Celtic then had to weather a storm of another kind, when Ujpest came at them straight from the start. However, by the 20th minute they had settled, and took a fortunate lead when Horvath diverted a Jim Brogan shot past his own 'keeper. Horvath redeemed himself in the second half, when he equalised with a magnificent long range shot, but as the game wore on Celtic actually looked stronger. After forcing five corners in quick succession, Lou Macari scored the winning goal ,with a deft lob over the Ujpest goalkeeper.

There was much celebration at the end, with Jock Stein ecstatic about the performance of his young team. He told the press: *'At this level, when you consider the age of this team of ours, it is probably Celtic's best European display since Lisbon'*. Stein was also quick to point out that his *'Quality Street Gang'* graduates were still at the learning stage, and that McGrain aged 21, Connelly 23, Macari 22, Hay 23 and Dalglish 21, all had their best years well ahead of them.

The happy Celtic fans travelled back to the Duna Intercontinental hotel to enjoy Richard Burton's hospitality, with Burton declaring that the till would ring to the tune of £5,000 before the festivities would end. Burton and Taylor posed for photographs with Celtic scarves, and happily mingled amongst the Celtic fans, showing a great deal of modesty and humour. When one fan referred to Taylor as *'your majesty'*, she replied, *'No, that's the other Elizabeth.'*

Burton then had his audience cheering with a fine rendition of *'I belong to Glasgow'*. Only a week earlier the couple had entertained Princess Grace of Monaco, and now were entertaining Celtic supporters from Scotland. None of the Celtic fans had ever experienced a night like it, and were never likely to again.

On the flight back to Glasgow, Gerry McNee was delighted with his exclusive scoop for his newspaper. He had arranged for Elizabeth Taylor to be presented with a floral bouquet and a Celtic fan on the plane came and thrust money into his hand, as part payment for the flowers. McNee happily explained that the cost had been covered by his newspapers' expense account and there was no need for payment. However, the fan insisted he accept the cash, stating, *'I want to be able to tell them in my local that I bought flowers for Elizabeth Taylor.'*

Two days after returning from Budapest, Jock Stein took a call in his office from a Mr Jenkins, phoning from Wales. The caller turned out to be Richard Burton's brother, Jenkins being the family name, and he contacted the Celtic manager after receiving a call from Budapest. Richard had said how sorry he was that the players had missed the party, how he hoped to see Celtic play some time in the future, and what fine company the Celtic fans had been.

Aberdeen continued to be Celtic's main obstacle to another league title, but after New Year Celtic pulled away and had a five point lead when they travelled to Pittodrie on 11th March. Days before the game Aberdeen had chosen to sell their captain and biggest asset, Martin Buchan, to Manchester United for £120 000, then a record fee for the Old Trafford club. This angered the Dons' fans, and Celtic were happy to see out a 1-1 draw, knowing that their closest challengers were severely weakened following Buchan's departure. Kenny looked jaded at Pittodrie and was substituted during the game. There were now concerns that he was in danger of becoming burned out, having played so much football, and consequently Stein withdrew him from the Scottish League team who were to play the English League at Ayresome Park.

In the second leg against Ujpest Dozsa, in front of a crowd of 75,000, Celtic found the Hungarians to be a different proposition from the first game. Ujpest scored after only 5 minutes and gave the Celtic defence a torrid time for the rest of the half. Jock Stein's master stroke was to bring Jimmy Johnstone on as a substitute, and with the wee man on the park Celtic were able to up their game. A barrage of attacks rained down on the Ujpest goal until Lou Macari equalised, with a delicate lob, after a great George Connelly through ball from defence. The Belgian referee, Robert Schaut, stated afterwards that: *'No team in Europe could have stood up to the Celtic pressure in the second half. The effort that Celtic raised is something that I have never seen before.'*

In the semi final draw made in Geneva, Celtic found themselves paired with old adversaries, Inter Milan.

....

Celtic View reports on Canadian interest after the European Cup semi final draw.

Thousands of Celtic fans will be cheering their team against

Inter Milan from more than 4000 miles away. They'll be paying up to £5 a head to see Celtic in action in Toronto's Maple Leaf Ice Rink. A giant screen has been specially erected to show colour pictures via the Telstar satellite. The arena will be packed with 12,000 exiled Scots, Irish and Italians. The man behind the idea is Fergus McCann, a professor at Montreal University. The venture has cost him $40,000 - including hiring the satellite at $100 a minute. There will also be plenty of cheers for Celtic in other parts of the world, for at least nine countries are taking in the Inter semi final live from Parkhead. And top of the list is the Congo, one of the most soccer conscious countries in Africa. The Congolese who are pro-British are reported to be rooting for Celtic. Other countries taking the game live are Italy, Spain, France, Belgium, Greece and Russia.

Celtic View, 19th April 1972

It was now inevitable that Celtic would claim their seventh successive league title, and they did so in the quaint setting of East Fife's modest Bayview Park in Methil on 15th April. In a great gesture from the Fifers, Celtic ran out at Bayview to the familiar sound of *'You'll Never Walk Alone'* playing on the club's tannoy system. They went on to win 3-0. Kenny Dalglish won his first league winners medal, and it was much deserved, as he had played in 31 from a possible 34 games, scoring 17 goals.

Kenny then faced the two biggest games in his career thus far, when Celtic faced Inter Milan. In the first leg on 5th April, Celtic played a game of containment, restricting Inter to very few shots at goal. In the second leg, two weeks later, the Italians retreated into their familiar defensive shell and, after a bright start, Celtic struggled to break them down. Jimmy Johnstone was man marked by Tarcisio Burgnich and found it difficult to make space. As the game wore on extra time looked inevitable.

In the extra period Celtic resorted to playing high, hopeful balls into the Inter area which the Milan side coped with comfortably. The Celtic fans sang, *'All we are saying - is give us a goal!'*, to the tune of John Lennon's hit song, *'Give peace a chance'*, but to no avail. After 120 goalless minutes, a penalty shootout was required to decide the winners. Kenny had been replaced by Dixie Deans in the second half, as Celtic searched for a vital goal, and it was then decided that Dixie would take the first penalty.

As Deans walked to the penalty spot he passed Jimmy Johnstone, and he asked his team mate to say a *'wee prayer'* for him. To the despair of almost everyone in the 75,000 crowd, Deans hit his shot over the crossbar. Lido Vieri, Inter's goalkeeper, said afterwards: *'I used my head more than my hands when I saw it was the Celtic substitute to take the first kick. I could see he was nervous so I deliberately moved to put him off as he approached the ball to take his shot.'*

Vieri's trick worked and Inter had the advantage. All the other penalties were scored and Celtic were out, by virtue of a 5-4 scoreline. The irony was that Celtic had practiced penalties in training, and that Deans had been the most successful scorer during those sessions.

It's hard to describe the frustration that everyone associated with Celtic felt, having lost a game of this magnitude in such a cruel fashion. Jock Stein had allowed some seasoned professionals players to leave during the course of the season, and it was easy for critics to say that the experience of Tommy Gemmell, Willie Wallace and John Hughes could have been crucial in the games against Inter. Gemmell in particular, was renowned for his powerful shots from distance, and this could have been the vital key to unlocking the tight Inter defence. Inter lost 2-0 to Ajax in the final in Rotterdam, and many felt that Celtic would have been a more attractive prospect for Ajax in the final.

....

Alan Rough declares his love for Celtic.

I was a red hot Celtic fan. The year before Celtic won the European Cup I went with a pal to a Celtic-Rangers match and I became hooked on Celtic that day. I was playing with Sighthill Juniors then and I wasn't able to get to Saturday matches but I never missed a midweek fixture. Celtic's attacking style made their games a must for me. They always gave you your money's worth and they still do.

Celtic View, 19th April 1972

....

Jock Stein and his players had to recover quickly from such a huge disappointment, as they were to play Hibs in the Scottish Cup final on the last day of the season. There were rumours that Stein was considering leaving Kenny out of his final team, as he had looked tired towards the season's end. However, Stein kept faith in him and played Kenny in a midfield role alongside Bobby Murdoch and Tommy Callaghan. Celtic hit the heights during this match and won emphatically by 6-1. They faced a fine Hibs side, but on cup final day there were not many sides who could have coped with Celtic, when Murdoch, Connelly, Johnstone and Deans all hit top form. Deans, the villain of the piece against Inter, became an instant hero when he scored a hat trick. His second goal was a spectacular individual effort, and after scoring he performed an impromptu forward roll on the Hampden turf in celebration.

Jock Stein was delighted by the manner of the victory, as his team had played the attacking football he had so long advocated. He was also heartened by the 106,000 attendance, which was larger than the English cup final attendance at Wembley on the same day. The Celtic support was bolstered by hundreds of fans who had flown from Toronto, New York and New Jersey at great expense, to back their team in Scottish football's showpiece game.

Kenny was thought to be in the running for the Scottish football writers' player of the year, but the award was given to Dave Smith of Rangers. Smith was a fine player but it's remarkable that very few Celtic players were to win this award during the nine-in-a- row years, at a time when the Celts were so dominant in the Scottish game.

At the end of the season Kenny was delighted to travel again to the island of Bermuda, where Celtic played a couple of games, but were mainly able to relax and enjoy the weather after another exhausting, yet rewarding season. In June Scotland were invited to play in the Independence Cup in Brazil, a tournament to celebrate 150 years of Brazilian independence. Scots' manager Tommy Docherty was desperate for a number of Celtic players to go, and wanted Dalglish, Macari, Johnstone, Murdoch and McNeill to travel. Jock Stein thought it best that the players have a full summer's rest, and allowed only one Celt, Macari, to travel to Brazil. In Kenny's case he was best rested, but Johnstone, Murdoch and McNeill were all said to have regretted missing out on the opportunity of playing in front of 130,000 fans in the legendary Maracana stadium.

In the Celtic View's end of season review John McPhail made the following observations about Kenny's first full season in the first team: *'Kenny had a wonder start to the season. His displays against Rangers in the League Cup were positively brilliant for a boy with so little first team experience. He soon became a Scotland choice. Unfortunately the boy is the kind of player who exerts every ounce of energy in order to give a full ninety minutes for club and country. Not a bad complaint but when you play as many tough matches as Celtic do week in, week out, for the entire season then something must be left in reserve. Young Ken just didn't pace himself. Under the guidance of*

Jock Stein I suggest that the fans can look forward to more economy of effort from this brilliant lad and a consistency that will help us to go on to great things in Europe.'

Kenny had made the all important first team breakthrough and was now an established first team player. He was now to prove he was not a one season wonder.

CHAPTER SEVEN
HOLDING HIS OWN - 1972/1973

The start of season 1972-73 was very low key for Kenny and for Celtic. The League Cup draw put Celtic in a section with East Fife, Arbroath and Stirling Albion, a grouping which hardly caught the imagination of the fans. Kenny did create one record, when he became the only Celtic player to score in all six of the League Cup section games, a feat that has never been equalled. A fire at Celtic Park in August had destroyed 900 seats, requiring Celtic to play home league fixtures against Kilmarnock and Rangers at Hampden Park. Celtic were given a kick off time of 7pm for their game against Kilmarnock on Saturday 2nd September This was to accommodate lowly Queens Park, who had a traditional 3pm fixture on the same day. Saturday evening football did not prove to be an attractive proposition for the fans, with just 11,560 turning out to see Celtic win 6-2 .

Since the start of the season Kenny had appeared as part of a three man midfield, alongside Bobby Murdoch and Tommy Callaghan. He was playing this role when Celtic faced Rangers on 16th September. The game kicked off at 12 noon, in order to allow a few hundred hardy souls to watch Queens Park play Stranraer at 3.30. Rangers were proud holders of the European Cup Winners' Cup, having beaten Moscow Dynamo in May. They were keen to capitalise on their European success, with Celtic once again having given up home advantage for a big Glasgow derby.

The game was a mismatch, with Celtic running out easy winners. Kenny gave them the lead after only 2 minutes, scoring from a tap in after Jimmy Johnstone set him up. Kenny repaid the compliment in 17 minutes, when he created a goal for Johnstone, after a great run and cross. The game was as good as over when Lou Macari made it 3-0 after 50 minutes, and the Celtic fans roared with joy, *'We want seven!'* and *'Easy!...Easy!...'* The second half saw Celtic miss a series of chances in one of the most one sided Old Firm games ever.

A most curious scene arose in the final minute. Rangers' captain John Greig burst through to score with a fine shot, and as the ball hit the net at the Celtic end, the Celtic fans gave a huge, spontaneous cheer. There were very few Rangers fans left in the ground, and Greig acknowledged the roars of the Celtic fans with a *'salute'*. In truth, there were many Celtic supporters who respected Greig's fighting spirit, as his team mates appeared to have accepted their fate long before the end.

However, some Celtic supporters were later to lament this game, regretting that they had not put their rivals to the sword with a more comprehensive victory. There was the feeling that Rangers got off lightly that day. A succession of Celtic missed chances in the second half frustrated some fans. An anonymous Celtic supporter recalled the events of the day: *'I have great memories of this game. It was the most one sided Old Firm game I ever saw. Usually I don't relax at these games even with a couple of goals in the bag, but this one was different. After 20 minutes there was no doubt who was going to win. Celtic were simply far too good. The gulf between the teams was huge and we were knocking the ball around without breaking sweat while they were chasing shadows. Although we gave John Greig an ironic cheer when he scored, the funniest moment was a wee bit earlier. Colin Stein was having a real nightmare but at one point out on the left touchline he actually won a tackle. The Celtic fans gave him a cheer. He then went on a run down the wing and beat another Celtic player. More cheers from the Celtic fans. He continued his run, but then got the ball stuck between his feet causing him to fall over, while the ball went out for a shy to Celtic. Cue hysterical laughter from the Celtic End. I can still recall the reaction from one of my mates hanging over a crush barrier with tears of laughter all over his face. The whole Celtic End was one big smile. In later years I wished Celtic had really gone for it that day. We could have got seven or eight if we had pushed it. At the time though the feeling of euphoria from the mickey taking was wonderful. Problem is that all these years later people just see a score of 3-1 and don't realise how much we really thumped them. I also attended the game at Tynecastle when Hibs beat Hearts 7-0 in January 1973. That game is remembered as a trouncing for Hearts because of the scoreline, yet the gap between them and Hibs that day was nothing like the gap between us and Rangers that September day at Hampden.'*

Forty eight hours after their Old Firm victory Celtic travelled to Manchester to play in Bobby Charlton's testimonial game. A large group of supporters made the journey from Glasgow, and Celtic put on quite a show, despite the game finishing 0-0. From boyhood, Kenny had been a huge admirer of Denis Law, and after the final whistle he chased after Denis for his jersey. At the time Kenny said: *'I'm only sorry he was wearing no 8 and not his famous no 10 jersey that night. I was just like a lot of other wee Scottish boys who idolised Denis. If someone had told me then that one day I would play alongside him I would have thought they were daft.'*

Kenny may have been star struck by Law, but he wasn't overawed on the pitch. In an article for Shoot magazine from the period, Kenny actually named Manchester United as his favourite other football team. This may come as a shock for Liverpool fans who have a fierce rivalry with United, but in 1972 it appeared that Kenny's English allegiances lay firmly at Old Trafford.

On the European front, Celtic were expected to dispose of the

KENNY OF THE CELTIC

Norwegian champions Rosenberg comfortably. In the home tie they won 2-1, in a game they should have won convincingly. In the return leg in Trondheim, Rosenberg led 1-0 at half time, meaning Celtic faced elimination on the away goals rule. In the second half they finally found their form, and Kenny scored his first European goal, when Jimmy Johnstone went on a sparkling fifty yard solo run to set him up.

....

Celtic's hooped jerseys are in high demand in Norway.

There was no swapping of jerseys immediately after the win in Trondheim. Not because Rosenberg were bad losers but because of a UEFA ruling. The soccer bosses feel swapping on the pitch lowers the tone of the game. Now it must be conducted inside. But even in the pavilion the Norwegians were reluctant to swap shirts for Celtic's all green change outfit. They insisting on having Celtic's green and white hoops. 'This is the strip all the world associates with Celtic', a Trondheim player explained. Luckily Celtic had packed a set of hooped strips in the hamper and were delighted to oblige their Norwegian hosts.'

Celtic View, 1st October 1972

....

In the next round Celtic were drawn against their old adversaries, Ujpest Dozsa of Hungary. This time Celtic were at home for the first tie. In the first half Ujpest grabbed the lead through their captain, Ferenc Bene. In the second half Kenny Dalglish led the way in a Celtic comeback. He equalised with a fine goal, showing considerable composure to score in a crowded goalmouth. He then scored the winner with a firm header from a Lennox cross.

The second leg in Budapest was always going to be tough, but when Bobby Murdoch and Lou Macari were ruled out through injury, matters became even more difficult. A desperately poor start from Celtic saw Ujpest lead 3-0 after only 22 minutes. The Celtic defence struggled against the pace of the Ujpest attack, although in the second half Celtic made a game of it, with Dalglish hitting the bar and McNeill seeing his header cleared off the line. The result wasn't the only disappointment for the supporters back in Scotland. STV had arranged to show the early evening kick off live on television, but although cameras filmed the action and Arthur Montford's commentary could be heard, a fault in the cable between Budapest and Vienna meant that no pictures were transmitted in Scotland. The result in Hungary meant there would be no European football after New Year for Celtic, which was unusual for the club at this time.

Despite their Euro reversal, the Celtic fans were still right behind their heroes, as Kenny recalled of the time: *'Celtic fans are undoubtedly the best in Scotland. Their loyalty was frightening. I remember coming home after getting beat 3-0 in Hungary by Ujpest Dozsa, to face an away game at Motherwell. We felt down and tired, but when we got on the pitch the roar that greeted us made the hair rise on the back of my neck. The place was packed, with the vast majority wearing green and white.'* Kenny Dalglish Soccer Annual 1979

Kenny was maturing off the park as well as on it. He now sported a trendy, long hairstyle which was fashionable, but not so long as for Jock Stein to object to. Danny McGrain had now established himself in the Celtic first team and the two became inseparable. Denis Connaghan remembers them, *'sitting together on the bus travelling to away games reading Shoot and Goal magazines'*.

....

A presentation was made to Jock Stein to mark seven league wins in a row. It was organised by a group of Glasgow businessmen and the presentation was made in the Grosvenor hotel. Bill Shankly handed over to Mr Stein a stereo record player and treated the guests to a few characteristically crisp observations of the game. 400 people were in attendance.

Celtic View, 15th November 1972

....

On 15th November Kenny had the honour of scoring his first goal for Scotland, in a World Cup qualifier against Denmark at Hampden, as Scotland continued their fine progress en route to the 1974 World Cup finals.

Celtic fought their way through to the League Cup final, where they faced Hibernian. The game was to be played on 9th December, leading to criticism of the Scottish League for playing such an important game in the depths of winter. Kenny was in fine form, having scored spectacular goals against Motherwell and Hearts in two Celtic victories. He was therefore reckoned to be Celtic's main attacking threat to a Hibs side which had improved enormously under Eddie Turnbull, and would be looking for revenge after their 6-1 humiliation in May's Scottish Cup final. Hibs were in a rich vein of form, having beaten Rangers comprehensively in the semi final, in addition to beating Sporting Lisbon 6-1 at Easter Road in the European Cup Winners' Cup. On the day Hibs kept up their good form, and deservedly won the League Cup for the first time, by a scoreline of 2-1. Celtic's only consolation was in a fine finish from Dalglish near the end of the game.

If the Hibs defeat was bad, then matters were about to get worse. Just after Christmas, Jock Stein was admitted to hospital for a short period, having suffered chest pains. While he was recuperating Celtic lost the New Year fixture 2-1 to Rangers at Ibrox. Tommy Docherty was making a great impression with the Scottish national team, and in December 1972 the Doc deserted his post to take over the reins at relegation threatened Manchester United. Lou Macari then rocked Celtic by asking for a transfer, which was most ill timed given the problems facing the club. Docherty moved for Macari and United paid a Scottish record fee of £200,000 for the Celtic striker's services. Macari had become a regular in the Scotland side during Docherty's spell as manager. As a result his head appeared to have been turned, on hearing how much the Anglo-Scots players were earning down south, hence his request for a transfer. Macari was not allowed to depart until the Celtic manager was back in control at Parkhead, and Stein was scathing in the press after his departure - '*Macari would never been allowed to go had I believed his absence would have weakened our set up.*'

Kenny Dalglish enjoyed a close personal relationship with Stein, but there was one occasion when the Celtic manager was required to chide his star player, as John Burns explains: '*My father used to own the Carousel night club and restaurant in Motherwell and was great mates with Jock Stein (they went way back to when Stein was a player). One Saturday afternoon Celtic's game was postponed late due to frost in Glasgow. The players thought the big man would let them all off for the afternoon but Jock decided they should all go to Fir Park as Motherwell were Celtics next opponents. He told them to drive to my Dad's place where lunch would be laid on before the game. One of the last to arrive was Kenny, who had trouble finding the car park. Cue long haired Kenny in his trendy Afghan coat telling big Jock that they were some directions he had given him! Stein, unperturbed, told him to get seated and order his food. Minutes later Jock asked my Dad if he could use his office for a private meeting. He then took Kenny in there and my Dad who could overhear in the outside corridor, said Stein tore him to ribbons for the way he spoke to him in public. Cue a very apologetic young Kenny heading back to his seat*

When Stein sat down again he called a waitress and told her to see if the lads wanted a drink and take their order. All the older guys like McNeil, Johnstone, Murdoch and Deans ordered soft drinks. The young guys like Connelly, Hay and Davidson ordered pints of lager. Big Jock then got the waitress to point out who had ordered the beers. It was his way of finding who were the drinkers. He then told her send soft drinks all round.'

On 7th February, on a foul night at Rugby Park, Kenny missed a great chance to put himself into the history books. Celtic were leading 4-0 against Kilmarnock, when they were awarded a penalty in the final minute. Kenny stepped forward to take the kick, and the opportunity to score Celtic's 6000th league goal. He had already scored twice and looked set for his hat trick, only to see his shot crash off the crossbar. Bobby Murdoch was to achieve the honour, scoring Celtic's landmark 6000th goal three days later, against Partick Thistle.

Kenny was now an established player in the Scottish International team, and he was the only Celtic player chosen to play against England at Hampden on 14th February. The game was arranged to celebrate the SFA's centenary. It was later described as, '*the other Saint Valentine's day massacre.*' Scotland were trounced 5-0 on a bitterly cold night where the pitch was barely playable. Kenny escaped the fall out afterwards, having been one of Scotland's better players. Willie Ormond had just succeeded Tommy Docherty as Scotland manager, and there was a sharp contrast in style between the unassuming Ormond and the exuberant Docherty. Ormond seemed under pressure, after only one game as boss.

In the 1970's there was a close bond between footballers and the public at large. This is borne out by a tale that Norman Emerson, then a university student, tells from February 1973: '*Glasgow Students Charity Week was traditionally a time when students from the city's colleges and universities indulged in activities ranging from collecting for charity in outrageous costumes, to flour battles that sometimes got out of hand and required the attendance of the local constabulary. Part of the traditions of this week also involved a fancy dress ball and a magazine called YGORRA - full of dubious humour. Charity week also involved the 'kidnapping' of celebrities, for ransom donations. Notre Dame Teacher Training College in the west end of Glasgow was the scene for the kidnapping of Kenny Dalglish in 1973. A phone call was made to Celtic Park, explaining that we wished to kidnap Kenny, and was met at first by an astonished silence, followed by a firm refusal and an explanation that such arrangements were not possible, not even for charity. The call was then interrupted by a loud voice on the other end of the line, followed by a muffled conversation in the background. A bold voice then came on the phone – unmistakeably that of Jock Stein. 'Can you guarantee that there will be no students running onto the pitch at Saturday's home game?' There was no way that this could be guaranteed but nevertheless the condition was readily agreed. 'Okay, meet Kenny at the Beechwood Restaurant in King's Park after training today – 2.30 sharp.' Three of us then drove from the west end to the south side in an old battered green Hillman Imp to pick up Kenny from the restaurant. When Kenny emerged we introduced ourselves and told him the plan - that we would take him back to Notre Dame College where we would hold him for two hours until Celtic paid £50 to the Student Charity Fund. Kenny looked a bit bemused and became even more so when he caught site of the proposed mode of transport! We escorted Kenny into the common room at the college to sit in the middle of a large circle of students who proceeded to ask him questions about all things Celtic. While it would have been similar to what he would later experience many times at supporters' nights, this must still have been quite daunting for a young Kenny who was still in the early years at Celtic. There were signs, nevertheless, of a certain steeliness in his response when occasionally one of the students would ask him a 'daft' question. Oblivious to the fact that Kenny would have just eaten a quality meal in the Beechwood only an hour before, it was decided to provide him with some college hospitality – a scotch pie and beans, glass of coke and a selection of bourbon cream biscuits were proudly set before Kenny – not surprisingly they were still there uneaten when he left two hours later! Photographers arrived and the pictures of Kenny being kidnapped were taken and the ransom sum was duly paid by Celtic. The incident harks back to a time when Jock Stein had a say in almost every aspect of the club and would capitalise on every opportunity to create a positive image for Celtic.'*

....

The Celtic View reports on Kenny's old school mate and Celtic fan, Jim Watt.

One of the best boxing contests to be held in Scotland for many years was the recent British Lightweight championship bout between Ken Buchanan and Jim Watt. Jim lost the fight and his title, but his contribution to this memorable fight was considerable. He also has links with Celtic, one of which stretches a few years back. He was at the same school as Kenny Dalglish although he was a year ahead. Now Jim often watches his old school mate in action for Celtic and will also pay a visit to Celtic social club now and then.

Celtic View, 14th February 1973

....

Kenny was involved in another club versus country dilemma, when he was chosen to represent Scotland under 23's against Wales in Swansea in March. Jock Stein was livid with Willie Ormond over Kenny's selection, and there were similarities to a year previously, when Stein claimed that Kenny was exhausted through playing too many games. Stein also thought that appearing in an under 23 match was now beneath Kenny, as he had nothing to prove after almost two seasons of excellent performances. In the event Kenny played and scored in Scotland's 2-1 win.

At the turn of 1973 something strange had happened in Scottish football. Rangers had begun to win games, and lots of them. The Ibrox men won sixteen consecutive league games through winter and spring, and by 10th March Rangers had caught Celtic on points, joining them at the top of the table. Draws for Celtic against Partick, East Fife and Dundee United had allowed Rangers to pull level.

The game against East Fife at Bayview Park on 17th February is best remembered for Celtic missing three penalties in a 2-2 draw.

From the first spot kick, Bobby Murdoch hammered the ball against the bar and over. However, East Fife full back, Bobby Duncan, was in the area when the kick was taken so a retake was ordered. Jock Stein signalled for Harry Hood to take it, only for East Fife goalie, Ernie McGarr, to save athletically with his foot. The third penalty was missed in 87 minutes, when McGarr saved cleanly from Kenny.

....

Celtic fan James Burke had nothing to say after he was arrested at last Saturday's Scottish Cup semi final. The charge was 'bawling, shouting and committing a breach of the peace' on the terracing during the match with Dundee. James, 18, went quietly with the police and he spent the weekend in the cells waiting for the case to come up. Yesterday he sat in the dock at Glasgow Sheriff court. Near him sat a nun...a Sister of Charity who works in a special school James attended in Glasgow's Tollcross. She was there to act as interpreter, for James has been deaf and Dumb since birth. Yesterday his name wasn't even called in court. Defence solicitor, William McGlynn, said: 'Mr Burke has been freed on the instructions of the Fiscal.'

Daily Record, 10 April 1973

....

After their setback at East Fife, Celtic responded by winning six successive games. They then required a win in their last fixture to clinch their eight-in-a-row title. Celtic's final game of the season was to be played against Hibs at Easter Road, on 28th April. Hibs had been in contention for the title at the turn of the year, but a series of injuries had affected their form and they had fallen away. With the exception of Ibrox, Easter Road was still the toughest ground in the country to go looking for a victory, so any title triumph was far from guaranteed. An astonishing crowd of 45,446 turned out, with an estimated 40,000 of them cheering for Celtic. Since Lou

Macari's departure in January Kenny had been pushed into the Celtic attack, alongside Dixie Deans. They formed a highly effective partnership, sharing 31 goals between them, prior to Celtic's visit to Edinburgh. Dalglish's smooth style contrasted with Deans more physical approach, but they blended together extremely well, and it was this striking pair who did the damage to the Hibs defence. Deans scored twice and Dalglish once, sending the Celtic fans into raptures, and a new chant was created - *'Eight in a row - Eight in a row - Hello! - Hello!'*

The celebrations afterwards were joyous, with the streets around Easter Road a sea of green and white after the match. Thousands of Celtic fans took over the pubs of the capital until well into the evening in a celebratory atmosphere. Prime Minister, Harold Wilson, was emerging from the North British Hotel in Princes Street, just as a huge contingent of Celtic fans arrived at Waverley Station after the match. His ministerial car was parked outside and was getting rocked from side to side, with his security men unable to do anything. Apparently Wilson looked apprehensive, but then the Celtic fans started singing, *'Haaarold Wil-son, Haaarold Wil-son'*, at the top of their voices, leaving a relieved Harold smiling and waving.

Ian Archer summed up the happy atmosphere after the match in the Glasgow Herald: *'So in the end the Celtic players ran around Easter Road applauding their own fans and eventually they disappeared down the tunnel. Jock Stein was already in the dressing room when they arrived. Half an hour later, from the corridor underneath the stand, we could hear them singing the same songs as their supporters beforehand. Reluctant as I am to criticise Champions, it has to be said that they were equally as out of tune.'*

Goodwill messages poured in to hail Celtic's fine achievement, with Stein's great friend Bill Shankly sending his best wishes and jokingly remarking that, *'They'll have to stop that league!'* Stein

HOLDING HIS OWN - 1972/1973

then reciprocated by sending congratulations to Shankly, as his Liverpool team had clinched the English title on the same day. Stein was delighted to win what may have been his most difficult title of the eight so far, telling the press: *'We have come through a transitional period. What made me happy was that so many of our players came back at the right time - Hay, Callaghan and Lennox.'*

....

Jock Stein was recently presented with a box of After Eight chocolates by a grateful Celtic fan. He turned it over to find one word written in block capitals - NINE.

Daily Record, 4th May 1973

....

One week later Celtic and Rangers contested the Scottish Cup final. The Ibrox side, in their centenary season, were desperate to win some silverware to commemorate this landmark occasion, and this was their last chance for glory. It had long been complained that Hampden finals lacked the glamour of Wembley, and for this occasion it was decided that there should be a royal presence. Accordingly the Queen's cousin, Princess Alexandra, was invited to present the trophy to the winners.

Celtic started well, and Kenny gave them the lead with a well taken low shot. This would normally have been a cue for Celtic to go on to win well, but Rangers proved a strong team on the day. Derek Parlane equalised on his 20th birthday, and the second half was only seconds old when Alfie Conn gave Rangers the lead. Celtic fought back and George Connelly equalised from a penalty. Minutes later Jimmy Johnstone scored, but his goal was disallowed in a debatable offside decision, which was to rankle Celtic officials afterwards. Jim Brogan was injured in a collision, and was replaced by Bobby Lennox. The Celtic defence was still reorganising, when Tom Forsyth scored after Derek Johnstone's header hit the post. Rangers held on to win 3-2. Princess Alexandra was said to have confided in Jock Stein that the Hampden final had a better atmosphere than Wembley. A crowd of 122,714 were in attendance at Hampden, the last time the grand old ground was to record a six figure attendance.

To round off the season, Celtic travelled to Elland Road to play in Jack Charlton's testimonial game. The Leeds centre half, a notable World Cup winner, had been with Leeds United for an astonishing twenty one years. Both teams put on a tremendous show of football, with Celtic winning 4-3. Kenny scored Celtic's opening goal with a terrific shot, but Jimmy Johnstone stole the show with a superb winning goal, when he raced from the halfway line before scoring.

Jack Charlton wasn't usually an emotional man, but he broke down afterwards during his lap of honour, when he was given a rousing ovation by the Leeds and Celtic fans. Big Jack confessed that this was the first time he had shed tears since the Manchester United Munich air disaster of 1958, in which his brother Bobby had narrowly avoided death. After the match Kenny Dalglish was able to swap his jersey with Leeds' captain, Billy Bremner, the pair now well acquainted through playing together for Scotland.

....

The Evening Times reports on the aftermath of Jack Charlton's testimonial game, 9th May 1973

Pretty 19 year old Leeds barmaid Catherine Watson drowned her sorrows last night after Celtic had beaten her home team 4-3. And this morning she woke up penniless, stranded and hungry...in Glasgow. Catherine said, 'I don't know how I got here. I remember being in the Irish centre in Leeds and that's the last thing I remember. I went to the match to watch Jackie Charlton play his last game. Unfortunately Leeds lost and I had a bit too much to drink afterwards.' Glasgow police are trying to find a way of getting Catherine back home and her boss at the New Eagle Bar has agreed to stand security for her fare. 'I am supposed to working tonight,' said Catherine, 'but I don't think there is much chance of that.'

....

Kenny completed his season by playing in all three of Scotland's Home International matches. Willie Ormond was desperate for some good results, following the 5-0 thrashing from England in February. He paired Kenny and Rangers' Derek Parlane in attack for the game against Wales at Wrexham. The duo were described as the best strike partnership in the country, and helped Scotland to a well deserved 2-0 win. Three days later Northern Ireland achieved a surprise 2-1 win at Hampden, with Kenny scoring Scotland's goal after a great overlap by Danny McGrain.

The visit to Wembley in 1973 was Kenny's first appearance on that hallowed turf, and it was not to be his last. England won 1-0, but the game is perhaps best recalled for a stunning save by England goalkeeper, Peter Shilton. With only five minutes remaining, Kenny struck a perfect left foot volley and the ball headed goalwards, only for Shilton to launch himself across goal, diverting the ball with one hand. Shilton later confessed that he could not recall making a better save for England.

Kenny could then reflect on a difficult but successful season. He had scored forty two goals for club and country, and had become a popular choice for Celtic and Scotland. He was now a successful international class footballer and further success was on the horizon.

CHAPTER EIGHT
VERGE OF GREATNESS - 1973/1974

Kenny Dalglish did not have a long break from football during the summer of 1973, much to Jock Stein's frustration. In late June Scotland lined up two friendlies against Switzerland and Brazil, and Kenny played in both. Scotland lost 1-0 in Berne to the Swiss. Whilst few Scotland fans will recall this scoreline, they will be more likely to remember George Connelly's much publicised walkout at Glasgow Airport, as the team awaited their flight.

One week later the Scots faced Brazil at Hampden. This was only three years after the Brazilians won the World Cup, but the South American's were a disappointment, missing the flair of the recently retired Pele, Gerson and Tostao. Scotland gave a good account of themselves, and were unlucky to lose through a Derek Johnstone own goal.

Back at Parkhead Jock Stein was looking to change the shape of his team. He had already been busy in the transfer market, bringing some new recruits to Celtic. In January he had purchased Kilmarnock goalkeeper Alistair Hunter for £50,000. Hunter then played a major part in Celtic's title success during the closing months of the season, and he also established himself as Scotland's first choice goalkeeper.

In February Stein had brought Hearts' left winger Andy Lynch to Parkhead, for a fee of £35,000. Lynch had found it hard to break into the side, but following pre-season training he was said to be raring to go. Midfield man Steve Murray was a surprise £50,000 signing from Aberdeen at the end of the season. Murray had been coveted by several English sides, and it was seen as a coup for Celtic when they managed to attract him to Parkhead.

All of the new signings were chosen for Celtic's three games in the Drybrough Cup tournament, but it was another new face who was grabbing the headlines. Eighteen year old midfielder Brian McLaughlin was described as the most talented teenager that Jock Stein had ever come across. So much so that Stein had decided against sending McLaughlin on loan to a junior team, as was the norm for Celtic youngsters at the time. Instead he placed him directly into reserve football. McLaughlin, a talented and graceful player, looked so capable at that level that Stein now had no hesitation in promoting him to the first team.

En route to the Drybrough final Celtic thrashed Dunfermline 6-1 and Dundee 4-0, both ties played at Celtic Park. In the Dundee game, McLaughlin scored an outstanding goal when he ran across the face of the penalty area, before swivelling and hitting a glorious shot from twenty yards. The Celtic fans must have hoped it was a taste of things to come. He was regarded as similar in style to Dalglish, and his link play with Kenny was absolutely outstanding, a fine example of how great players can easily make a connection on the field of play. In the final at Hampden Celtic were unlucky to lose 1-0 to Hibs, after extra time. For Stein, the Drybrough tournament proved to be a worthwhile exercise, with Hunter, Murray, McLaughlin and Lynch all looking impressive.

Penarol of Uruguay visited Celtic Park for a prestigious pre-season curtain raiser. Bill Shankly was a guest of the club for this fixture, and Celtic chose to mark the occasion by giving him a presentation to mark his recent success at Liverpool. Shankly was always held in the highest regard by Celtic supporters. He had been the only top division English manager to take the trouble to travel to Lisbon in

1967, when Celtic became the first British club to lift the European Cup. Shankly was presented with an inscribed clock with the message, *'To Bill Shankly - for victory season 1972/73 - from Celtic football club.'* Celtic and Penarol lined up to give the Liverpool manager a guard of honour on to the field, and the Celtic crowd roared - *'Shankly!... Shankly!..'.* The great man, in turn, saluted the supporters. He enjoyed himself so much it took some time to coax him away from the Jungle enclosure. Afterwards an emotional Shankly told the Celtic View: *'It was a magnificent gesture for Celtic to even consider making a presentation to me. As for the Celtic fans, their reception gave me an even greater thrill if that was possible. It's the men who stand on the terracings and sit in the stand who make professional football possible and their welcome for me was out of this world. The clock itself is something I shall always treasure but the thought behind it is something I shall cherish as long as I live. To be honest I was very nervous and excited before the presentation, even a little overawed. But during the ceremony when I heard the crowd I felt so much at home I felt as if I was standing in front of the Anfield Kop. Let's hope that Celtic and Liverpool meet in the European Cup final this season. What a night that would be.'*

Celtic beat Penarol with an impressive display and Kenny scored another sensational goal, for which he was rapidly becoming famous. In the second half he received the ball twenty yards from goal, looked up and delicately placed a glorious shot over the despairing Penarol 'keeper.

The League Cup section paired Celtic with Rangers yet again. This time two teams were to qualify from each group, which took a bit of the sting out of the two Old Firm encounters. In the first game at Ibrox Celtic won 2-1, with late goals from Hood and Lennox. In their home tie, Celtic played Rangers off the park in the first half, and a 1-0 lead was scant reward for their domination. In the second half a series of controversial decisions affected Celtic's rhythm, and Rangers scored three times. Jimmy Johnstone was also ordered off in a game Celtic should never have lost.

The start of the league season saw terracing admission prices rise from 33p to 35p. The Celtic fans could not complain about the increase, as they were being royally entertained by a team playing attacking football in the great Celtic tradition. The League flag was unfurled at home to Clyde on 8th September, in a game where every Celtic player wore the no 8 shorts to commemorate eight League titles in succession. The entire afternoon had a gala day feel to it and Celtic won 5-0. However the win came at high cost, when Brian McLaughlin sustained a horrendous knee injury in a brutal tackle from a Clyde defender. Jock Stein was said to have been horrified when he saw the extent of the damage to McLaughlin, and although Brian returned to the game he was never to completely fulfil his early potential.

Celtic returned to Ibrox, this time on league business, on 15th September. Kenny had been doubtful due to an ankle injury, and although Stein had stated he wasn't completely fit, he was selected as McLaughlin and Lennox were themselves out through injury. Kenny courageously played through the pain barrier and got his reward when Jimmy Johnstone scored a second half winner with a diving header. The Celtic fans had a popular, if slightly crude, chant for Kenny which was loudly sung to the tune of 'McNamara's band':

Oh his name is Kenny Dalglish, he's the leader of our team
The finest centre forward that the world has ever seen
He's here, he's there, he's everywhere, to score a vital goal
And as for Derek Parlane you can stick him up your ★★★★

....

Shoot magazine from 1973 reports on Policing costs.

The cost of keeping law and order at a Celtic-Rangers clash is to have 500 policemen on duty. The Scottish police have a flat rate for their services for these games.

Constable - £1.65 Sergeant - £1.95 Inspector - £2.25

Chief inspector - £2.45 Superintendents - £2.70

In addition each police horse costs 32p per hour, which makes football in Glasgow very expensive.

....

After the match the Celtic players were to hear some sad news, as Kenny was later to recall, in Robert Harvey's book about Bobby Murdoch: *'We had just beaten Rangers at Ibrox and were cock-a-hoop in the dressing room. Then the boss announced that Bobby Murdoch was going down to Middlesbrough for signing talks. The celebrations just died. I am sure there were lumps in all the boys' throats. Nobody wanted to see Bobby leave but it was a great gesture from a great club to a great player to give him the reward of a free transfer for such long and loyal service.'*

Murdoch had been a tremendous servant to Celtic, but had lost his place in midfield to new signing Steve Murray. Bobby had played an integral part in Kenny's development, and there was genuine disappointment at departure, felt by players and supporters alike.

In late September the country became World Cup mad, as Scotland prepared to face Czechoslovakia in a World Cup qualifier at Hampden. A win would see the Scots qualify for the first time since 1958. They now had the perfect opportunity to get to the finals, with home advantage and a crowd in excess of 95,000 to roar them on. Celtic provided five of the starting eleven - Hunter, McGrain, Connelly, Hay and Dalglish, which was a great source of pride for Jock Stein. The *'Quality Street Gang'* had graduated, and the cream of the crop were now making their mark in the international team.

The Czechs opened the scoring when Ally Hunter blundered, allowing a speculative shot from Nehoda to slip through his hands. Sadly, this was a blow from which Hunter was to never truly recover, and his career went rapidly downhill afterwards. Jim Holton equalised before half time, and in the second half Scotland pressed the Czechs back into defence. Dalglish was still not fully fit and he was withdrawn for Joe Jordan, as Willie Ormond looked for more of an aerial threat in attack.

The substitution was inspired. In the 75th minute Jordan scored with a firm header, after a wonderful, swerving cross from Willie Morgan. A new Hampden roar was born when the old ground exploded with the cheers of the crowd. Scotland held on to win 2-1, to be followed by joyous celebrations. Manager Ormond and captain Bremner were launched high on the shoulders of the players, and paraded around Hampden. Old war horses Bremner and Law were unashamedly in tears with the emotion of it all. The Celtic quintet were in the younger age bracket, and it would be many years later before they would fully appreciate the magnitude of what was achieved that night.

A few weeks later Scotland lost 1-0 in their final game, a now meaningless fixture against the Czechs in Bratislava. On the same night, Poland defied the might of England at Wembley. They achieved a 1-1 draw, qualifying for the finals at England's expense. Scottish newspapers reported on a buoyant Scotland squad making the journey home, especially the Anglo players, who would have bragging rights over their English club colleagues. Manchester United's Willie Morgan even threatened to wear his Scotland jersey to club training, to remind his English colleagues that Scotland were Britain's only representatives in West Germany.

Hearts were the early season pace setters in the Scottish league, and a crowd of 33,000 packed into Tynecastle in October when Celtic came calling for a top of the table clash. Stein's men proved too strong, with Celtic winning 3-1, having been three up at half time. Dalglish was now being described as not only a great goal scorer, but a scorer of great goals. His brace at Tynecastle showcased the tremendous variety of his scoring ability - the first, a cool finish having being sent clear on goal, and the second, a spectacular diving header. Celtic moved to the top of the table and were to stay there for the rest of the season.

In the European arena Celtic toiled to get past the Danish champions, Vejle. The Danes arrived in Glasgow with a warning for the Celts, having caused a major upset by beating French champions, Nantes, in the first round. In the first game Celtic were captained by Jimmy Johnstone. It was a dull goalless draw, during which Vejle employed a very capable defensive system which Celtic were unable to break down. In the return game in Denmark a Bobby Lennox goal gave Celtic a narrow victory, and a passage to the quarter finals.

As autumn descended Jock Stein was eager to improve his squad. He made bids for Dundee striker John Duncan and Crystal Palace defender Iain Phillip. Stein was so keen to recruit Duncan that he offered the Dens Park club a fee, plus the choice of Harry Hood, Jimmy Quinn or Vic Davidson in part exchange. Dundee held out for a straight cash transaction, and Spurs eventually paid £150,000 for Duncan's services. Stein was also said to be interested in Alan Gordon of Hibs and Jim McCabe of Motherwell, but neither player made the move to Celtic.

In late 1973 Celtic midfielder Davie Hay went on strike after being in dispute with the club. Hay was unhappy that bonus payments were not paid to players who were injured whilst playing for Celtic. The club were not noted for paying high salaries, but had an excellent bonus scheme, which was payable only to those who played. Hay's close pal George Connelly came out in support of his team mate, but was soon persuaded back. Hay eventually returned to the fold, just before the League Cup semi final against Rangers in early December.

It was to be a timely return, as Hay helped Celtic to a memorable 3-1 victory. The hero of the hour was Harry Hood, who scored a perfect hat trick of right foot, left foot and header. Hood had just declined a move to Dundee, and on this performance the fans were delighted he had stayed with Celtic. Harry had even seen a fourth goal disallowed, after a rather contentious offside decision.

Dalglish played the role of provider in this game, making two of Hood's goals, and giving a superb display of intelligent movement and ball control in difficult conditions. The game was played on a night of vile weather, with the Celtic fans completely exposed to the elements on Hampden's open terraces. Despite suffering in the wind and rain, the Celtic fans displayed an element of good humour at 3-1, spontaneously belting out Gene Kelly's famous song - *'We're singing in the rain, we're happy again, just singing and dancing in the rain.'*

This victory over Rangers took Celtic through to the League Cup final against Dundee. The game was to be played at Hampden just ten days before Christmas. This was a time of strife and the country was sliding into a depression. Power cuts, strikes and rampant inflation were making the headlines, as the government instituted the *'Three Day Week'*. A ban on generators saw the game hastily rescheduled from 3.00 to 1.30, avoiding the use of floodlights, and thus conserving energy during the power shortage. Supporters experienced transport problems due to a fuel shortage, and consequently very few Dundee fans managed to make it from Tayside to Glasgow.

If this wasn't bad enough, the weather on the morning of the game was to make matters even worse. Sleet had fallen on an icy pitch, meaning that some areas of the field were hard whilst other parts held surface water. Referee Bobby Davidson inspected the pitch and declared it playable, to the dismay of Jock Stein and Dundee manager, Davie White. At kick off 27,974 hardy souls had braved the elements, a desperately poor attendance for a Hampden final. Had the game been held back until spring, a crowd of around the 70,000 could realistically have been expected.

Celtic played poorly and lost 1-0 with ex-Celt, Tommy Gemmell, lifting the cup for Dundee. This was the fourth consecutive League Cup final Celtic had lost, and the media spoke of hoodoos and jinxes affecting Celtic in Hampden finals.

Celtic licked their wounds from their cup defeat, and started the New Year in fine style. In January they defeated Rangers 1-0 at Parkhead, courtesy of a Bobby Lennox goal, but their superiority should have been rewarded by a greater margin. Dalglish was, '*the game's class attacker*', having been at the heart of all Celtic's best moves. The Celtic fans lapped up yet another win over their great rivals, and the Jungle enclosure sang the following words to the Carpenters' popular chart hit, '*On Top of the World*'.

We're on the top of the league
Looking down on the Rangers
And the only explanation we can find
Is the team that we've got
Is the best team of the lot
And they've put us on the top of the league

Times were changing, within Scottish football and in the country in general. Sunday 27th January 1974 is a significant date in Scottish football. It marked the first occasion on which football was played on a Sunday afternoon. For their Scottish Cup tie Celtic played host to Clydebank. Dixie Deans became the first footballer to score on a Sunday when he gave Celtic the lead after four minutes, on the way to a 6-1 win. The experiment was deemed a success, with Celtic attracting 28,000 for a game against lowly opposition. However, it would be a few years later before Sunday games would become the norm.

Celtic lost two consecutive league games to Dundee and Motherwell in early February, allowing Hibs to narrow the gap at the top of the table to three points. Hibs were in good form and had brought Scottish striker Joe Harper back from Everton to boost their title bid. They paid a Scottish record fee of £120,000 for the ex-Aberdeen man. Hibs chairman Tom Hart was desperate for them to win the league title.

On a cold, crisp day 48,554 spectators packed into Easter Road to watch the two best teams in the country. Sunday Mail columnist and Hearts fan, John Fairgrieve, courted controversy by declaring that he wanted Hibs to beat Celtic. His reasoning was that a close title race would be good for Scottish football, and that Hibs' deserved some success for the quality of football that they played. This only served to inspire the Celtic players, and also ensured that the fans backed their team more loudly than ever. Celtic just had the edge and ran out winners by 4-2. It was an exciting game, with Kenny scoring Celtic's second goal after playing a fine one-two with Dixie Deans. The Celtic fans had a new anthem for their goal scoring striker - *'Kenny...Kenny Dalglish...everyone knows his name!'* This was sung to the tune of the popular kids' TV show, *'Rupert Bear'*. It was a very catchy chant and was sung for a considerable period around grounds in Scotland when Celtic fans were hailing their goal scoring hero.

This result set Celtic up nicely for their trip to Switzerland, where they were to face Basle in the European Cup quarter final, first leg. They looked to be in total control when Paul Wilson gave them the lead with a spectacular volley. Injuries to goalkeepers Hunter and Connaghan led to Evan Williams making a return to first team duty. Williams hadn't played first team football since January 1973, and looked rusty on the night. Before half time he allowed a weak shot from Ottmar Hitzfeld to slip under him, then stood and watched as Karl Odermatt's long range free kick flew into the net, all within the space of two short minutes. In the second half Celtic fought back, and Dalglish scored a terrific goal, coolly lifting the ball past the Basle 'keeper following great work by Danny McGrain. At 2-2 Celtic would have been happy, but Williams' night of misery was completed when he caused a penalty after a poor kick out. Hitzfeld, who would manage Borussia Dortmund to success in the Champions League final against Juventus in 1997, gleefully fired home the spot kick, making the score 3-2 to Basle. Jimmy Johnstone was injured for this match, and STV kindly allowed the wee man to watch the footage live from Basle before they edited it for highlights to be shown later that night.

....

Paul Wilson earned himself £4 when he scored against Basle. Celtic director Kevin Kelly drew Paul in the press box sweep and had gone straight to the dressing room to tell the player 'score the first goal and I'll share my prize'. And he did too.

Sunday Mail, 3rd March 1974

....

In the second leg, played at Parkhead on 20th March, Celtic made a whirlwind start and were 2-0 up after 15 minutes. Kenny opened the scoring with a header from Hood's in swinging corner, and then combined with Steve Murray to set up the second goal for Deans. Tragically, George Connelly broke his leg and was carried from the field. This injury was a devastating blow for Connelly, and was to deprive him of the opportunity of showcasing his talents in the forthcoming World Cup tournament.

Without Connelly Celtic's defence looked vulnerable, and they lost two soft goals before half time, giving Basle the aggregate advantage. In the second half Celtic attacked constantly, and Tommy Callaghan's fine volley took the match to extra time. With penalty kicks looming, Celtic made the vital breakthrough. A Basle defender's headed clearance fell to Steve Murray eight yards out and he calmly sent a looping header high into the net. Afterwards Murray said the goal came naturally to him, as he had practiced *'double headers'* as a boy in his school playground.

Kenny's efforts against Basle did not go unnoticed. In a Sunday Mail interview, his old Rangers hero, Jim Baxter, declared that Kenny was one of the few players he would pay to watch play in the modern game, and spoke about him in glowing terms: *'Young Kenny is a football genius. He is one of the great players in Britain and will get even better. He not only has panoramic vision which lets him take in the whole field in front of him, he can also see what's going on behind him.'*

....

The Celtic View reports on supporting Celtic from abroad.

One very keen Celtic fan missed the Basle game at Celtic Park because he couldn't get the time off work. Nothing unusual about that except that this fan is Christian Villemagne and he lives in St Louis in France. He was in Basle for the first leg and met George Gunnion of Dennistoun. But Christian had the consolation denied to Celtic fans who couldn't get to the game at Parkhead. He saw the game live on French TV.

Celtic View, 3rd April 1974

....

As the season came down to the wire Kenny was again believed to be in the running for the Scottish Player of the Year award. However, the football writers surprised everyone by giving a collective award to the Scotland World Cup squad, so Kenny missed out once again.

The crucial part of the season was now approaching, with Celtic looking a certainty for the league title. They were also well in the running for the European Cup and the Scottish Cup. The European Cup semi final draw paired them with Atletico Madrid. Alarm bells began to ring when it was realised that Atletico's manager was the notorious Argentinian, Juan Carlos Lorenzo.

Lorenzo had gained a reputation as a coach who employed dubious tactics in order to achieve results. This was highlighted in the 1966 World Cup, when England manager Alf Ramsey branded Lorenzo's Argentina side as *'animals'*. If that wasn't bad enough, Atletico's left back was Ruben Diaz, who had played for Racing Club against Celtic in the infamous World Club championship games in 1967. Racing Club severely provoked Celtic over two legs with their rough house tactics, which eventually resulted in all out warfare in the third and deciding match, played in Montevideo.

Prior to the first leg against Atletico, Real Madrid's West German star, Gunter Netzer, speaking in the Sunday Mail, described Atletico as follows: *'They get more luck than any team I've ever played against. They all want to play but they can fight for the ball.'* This would prove to be an understatement.

A crowd of 73,000 fans packed into Parkhead on 10th April for the first leg, with a huge media entourage arriving from the continent. They would have plenty to write about, but not for good reason. Celtic's fears with regard to Lorenzo's rough house tactics were quickly realised. From the kick off Atletico fouled, tripped, hacked, pulled jerseys and obstructed Celtic players all over the pitch. The referee was Dogan Babacan from Turkey. The poor man looked out of his depth, but nothing could have prepared him for what he endured at Celtic Park that night.

Jimmy Johnstone was the player targeted most for physical treatment and he suffered a series of brutal tackles. When Atletico players were punished by the referee they stood with heads bowed and hands clasped behind their backs, like naughty schoolboys being chided by their teacher. One of the worst culprits was Ruben Ayala. He was a player with flowing black locks and facial hair, and bore a remarkable resemblance to the cavalier character on McEwan's beer cans of the time. Atletico committed fifty fouls and had seven men booked. In the second half Babacan was required to send off Ayala, Diaz and Quique, all in the space of seventeen minutes. In terms of fairness, it should be pointed out that Jim Brogan and Dixie Deans were also booked.

Chances were few and far between. In the first half Celtic were unlucky when Harry Hood rounded the Atletico keeper, Miguel Reina, to cut the ball back for Kenny Dalglish to score. However, a linesman declared the ball had gone marginally out of play before Hood's cut back. TV footage later proved this was the wrong decision. In the second half Hood came close with a header and Dalglish saw Reina save his headed effort. The Madrid side were one red card away from the game being abandoned and curiously, despite the chaos going on around him, Barbacan only allowed for 15 seconds of injury time to be played. The game ended goalless and Atletico celebrated gleefully at the end. Even after the final whistle there was an altercation in the tunnel, when rival players threw punches and the police were needed to keep them apart.

Celtic players and supporters were praised afterwards for showing restraint in the face of severe provocation. However, the team were criticised for not putting Atletico to the sword when they were reduced to eight men late in the game, and reduced to defending grimly within their own eighteen yard box. Denis Connaghan was Celtic's goalkeeper, and he later recalled his experience in the Celtic View: *'One can hardly describe it as a football match, it was a shambles, and I wince even now over the brutal approach of Atletico and the abuse that Jimmy Johnstone in particular had to suffer. But the major memory of that evening is the remarkable restraint and self discipline of the Celtic players, and the fans, in the face of quite naked provocation.'*

The media reaction to the proceedings on the field of play was to make interesting reading, and was not complimentary to the Madrid side. Newspaper photos showed a semi naked Jimmy Johnstone, who posed to display the extent of the bruising and cuts he suffered during the course of the game at the hands of Atletico players. The Scottish newspapers described Atletico in banner headlines as *'beasts'* and *'savages'*. The popular magazine World Soccer, reported: *'Up until the Parkhead first leg fiasco, Madrid had always thrown up visions of the legendary Real with Di Stefano gliding through the centre, Gento sweeping magnificently down the wing, Puskas and his lethal shooting power, the towering defensive work of Santamaria. One giant, ugly, clumsy foot has trodden these cherished memories well and truly into the dirt.'*

Irish Celtic fan, J.A. McConville, was secretary of the Dublin Celtic supporters club, and he felt so aggrieved regarding the events of the game that he hand delivered the following letter to the Spanish Embassy in Dublin: *'I am making a formal protest on behalf of the Dublin branch of the Glasgow Celtic supporters club regarding the savage behaviour of your countrymen at last night's so called football match. Our supporters club travelled to see a football game, but were subjected to one of the worst exhibitions of animal savagery ever witnessed on a football field. The trouble was brought about by the team and officials of Atletico Madrid and we never thought it possible of a Spanish team. They started to brawl from the first whistle and continued even after the game and must therefore rank as one of the worst teams to leave Spain. I trust this protest will be lodged in the appropriate place.'*

The Spanish media had a different take on proceedings. Spain was still under the rule of General Francisco Franco, a fascist leader and ardent Spanish nationalist. It is perhaps in view of this that Spanish newspapers chose to portray Atletico as the victims in Glasgow. They ludicrously claimed that the Madrid side were the victims of a concerted campaign against them at the hands of Celtic, the referee and even the Glasgow police. Controversial journalist John Fairgrieve, writing in the Sunday Mail, actually compared the near hysterical Spanish press reaction to Nazi propaganda.

He went on to cite two neutral sources in support of Celtic. Jean Gaillard of France Soir said: *'The Spaniards alone where responsible for all the incidents and fouling that took place. They used every trick forbidden in football.'* The London Times football correspondent, Geoffrey Green, stated: *'The Spanish tactics were cynical and cruel. There was nothing in the black book they did not turn to. Their craze for power and money goes beyond reason and decency...the effigy of football is burned.'*

Fairgrieve also pointed out that Celtic had an exemplary disciplinary record in European football. In the fifty one European Cup ties played by Celtic since 1966, only Bobby Murdoch had been ordered off, and that had been for dissent, in Kiev in 1967.

It took a long time for the dust to settle after this match. Atletico were reported to UEFA for their misbehaviour, and at one point there was optimism that they could be banned from the tournament, and Celtic given a passage to the final. However, after a meeting in Geneva Celtic were informed they were required to fulfil their obligation by playing the second leg in Madrid.

On 24th April 1974 Celtic marched into the lion's den of Atletico's Vincente Calderon stadium for the second leg. Before the game Jock Stein and Jimmy Johnstone had received death threats, which must have been very distressing. Denis Connaghan later told the Celtic View what went on before the game even started: *'Madrid was an experience. We were virtually locked up in our hotel rooms for three days with armed guards round the place and they escorted us to and from training. The usual shopping expeditions were out and so we sat around the hotel playing cards and chess. It was hardly the ideal preparation for a semi final in the European Cup. A swimming pool in the hotel provided a bit of a diversion but one couldn't be rid of the 'cooped-up' feeling. It was one trip from which the families of Celtic players didn't get any souvenirs and my own impressions of what I'm told is a beautiful city are confined to glimpses from coaches going to and from the airport, the training ground and the stadium. The Spanish fans' gestures told us exactly what to expect at the aptly named Calderon stadium. It was a cauldron. You could almost feel the hostility coming from their fans towards us. Atletico continued the war of nerves. They wouldn't allow Celtic to loosen up on the pitch before the game. Not even on the touch lines. We were sent off to the dressing rooms.'*

One thousand armed police were estimated to be on guard, with water cannons and tear gas at the ready. In the first half Celtic played controlled football, and came close to scoring when McNeill narrowly headed over. Dalglish then saw his low shot saved by Reina. Atletico, who were on their best behaviour, pressed Celtic back as the game wore on. For 75 minutes Celtic held out, until Garate found space in the Celtic area to score. The Celts then attacked desperately, looking for the away goal which would win them through, only for Adelardo to score with 4 minutes remaining, clinching a 2-0 victory for the Spaniards.

Atletico's keeper on the night was Miguel Reina. His son, Pepe Reina, was Liverpool 's goalkeeper during season 2011-12, when Kenny Dalglish managed the Anfield side. It would be interesting to know if the two ever discussed those controversial Celtic - Atletico encounters from 1974.

Atletico were fined £14,000 for their antics at Celtic Park, but gained the reward of a place in the final, to be played in Brussels against Bayern Munich. To the frustration of all decent football fans, Atletico were only seconds away from winning, when Hans-Georg Schwarzenbeck dramatically equalised for Bayern in extra time, earning his side a replay. In the second game Bayern thrashed Atletico 4-0. Genuine football fans must surely have felt that justice had been done.

Three days after their Spanish ordeal Celtic faced Falkirk at Brockville, requiring a point to achieve their much coveted ninth successive league championship. Relegation threatened Falkirk

KENNY OF THE CELTIC

put up a fine show, holding Celtic to a 1-1 draw. Dalglish once again was Celtic's inspiration, scoring with a glorious shot from the edge of the area. At the end of the match happy Celtic fans invaded the park to salute the players and their heroes completed a lap of honour around Brockville. The old chant was updated as the fans sang - *'Nine in a row...nine in a row...hello!.. hello!'* However, these celebrations did not compare to those of previous title wins. Pictures from the day show Celtic players with haunted looks on their faces as they ran round Brockville. The mental scars from Atletico were evident and would take far longer to heal than any physical ones.

Celtic rounded off their season by playing Dundee United in the Scottish Cup final at Hampden. United's young manager Jim McLean courted controversy before the game, claiming that Celtic had only two players of genuine class - Kenny Dalglish and Danny McGrain. This may have served as an incentive to the Celtic players, as on the day they won by 3-0. The two main men were Harry Hood who scored the opening goal, and red shirted goalkeeper, Denis Connaghan, who defied Andy Gray at 2-0, when a United goal could have brought them back into the game. At the end of the match the sound of the Celtic fans celebrating in the Hampden north stand reverberated around the old stadium - *'Oh when the Celts, go marching in...oh when the Celts go marching in...I wanna be in that number...oh when the Celts go marching in!'*

....

The SFA try to get tough on Cup Final celebrations.

The one touch of occasion was predictably enough provided by the Celtic players after their decisive 3-0 victory over Dundee United. The 'no lap of honour' edict by the SFA was tossed aside as, before receiving the trophy from Lord Hughes, Billy McNeill led the players in an impromptu trot to both ends of the ground to thank their fans for their support throughout the season. This gesture was condemned by SFA secretary Willie Allan. 'It wasn't in the rules and it won't happen again.'

Evening Times, 6th May 1974

....

The Home Internationals saw Scotland play all three of their games at Hampden, with Kenny selected for all three fixtures. The first game was a disappointing defeat against Northern Ireland. However a 2-0 win against Wales featured Kenny as one of the goal scorers, setting the team up nicely for the big clash against England. A crowd of 94,000 fans turned up at Hampden on a wet afternoon, with England keen to make an impression, having failed to qualify for the World Cup finals. Scotland turned in a superb performance, with Kenny playing as part of a three man midfield, alongside Billy Bremner and Davie Hay. Scotland won 2-0 and if both goals could be described as slightly fortuitous, then it must also be said that Peter Shilton saved the English from an even heavier defeat.

This was Scotland's first win against England since 1967, and it sent them off to the finals in West Germany in fine spirits. In the newspapers Bill Dalglish was described as Kenny's biggest fan, and was reckoned to have watched every game his son had played in Scotland since primary school. Kenny was able to arrange for tickets and travel to West Germany for his Dad, which would have given him great satisfaction, in view of the sacrifices that his family had made in helping him along in his formative years. Kenny's mum Catherine also got in on the act, when the Sunday Mail ran a feature on *'World Cup mothers.'* The mother of each squad player was allowed to send a message of goodwill to their sons in West Germany, and Mrs Dalglish said of her boy: *'I'm proud of him and I know he'll live up to everyone's expectations.'*

Scotland's first game was against Zaire, and the Scots looked unsure as how to deal with the game. The Africans were an unknown quantity, and at 2-0 up in the second half Scotland sat on their lead, rather than chasing more goals.

In the next game against Brazil, Scotland performed heroically and should have won. Billy Bremner and Davie Hay won the midfield battle against Roberto Rivellino and Wilson Piazza, and with a little good fortune Scotland could have prevailed, but the game finished goalless.

The final game against Yugoslavia saw the Scots draw 1-1, meaning the Slavs and Brazil qualified from the group by virtue of goal difference. Scotland were unbeaten in the group but a shortage of goals against the whipping boys of Zaire in the first match had ultimately cost them dearly. They were the first team ever to be eliminated from the World Cup finals without losing a game.

By his own high standards Kenny's form had been disappointing at the World Cup. He was employed in midfield and had played with energy and enthusiasm, but the flair in his game had been missing. Kenny received a bit of media criticism, as he had been substituted in two of the three games, but later in *'King Kenny'* by Ken Gallagher, Scotland manager Willie Ormond showed he had not been disappointed: *'I consider Kenny to be one of the greatest players ever to kick a ball. All that nonsense about him not playing well for his country, not once do I think he let me down. He thought he did in the 1974 World Cup but I never thought that. When we went to West Germany it was a new adventure for every one of the players. No one had been to the finals before and there we were, in against Brazil and Yugoslavia both very difficult teams to face and no way was I disappointed with anyone's performance.'*

Kenny's failure to replicate his Celtic form for Scotland could have been down to his reservation around the experienced, more gregarious personalities, such as Denis Law and Billy Bremner.

Scotland team mate of the period, Sandy Jardine, commented in the Sunday Mail: *'The point about it is that Kenny would not push himself whilst in the company of those Scottish players who were regarded as the elder statesmen of the time. At Celtic he would have been familiar with everyone on a daily basis but when it came to the business of international get togethers Kenny was inclined to say nothing and think a lot.'*

Another Scotland team mate of the period, Pat Stanton, remembers Kenny impressing his international colleagues in other ways: *'If you were ever in Billy Bremner's company he was a dominant character, in training or before games. Kenny was quiet in comparison, but when the other players saw him in training they knew he was a player.'*

Perhaps the real reason Kenny didn't hit top form in West Germany was that he may have felt burnt out. In season 1973-74 he played an astonishing seventy four games for club and country, and he hadn't taken a serious break from football in the previous twelve months. It was to his credit that he wanted to play in every game for Celtic and Scotland, no matter the opposition.

Jock Stein had been in West Germany as a summariser for the BBC, and commentator Archie McPherson recalls the Celtic manager being tremendously enthusiastic about his star player before the events in West Germany. *'Jock kept building Kenny up so much so that Tony Queen and I thought, is he trying to sell him? Every interview he gave he was praising Kenny to the hilt, especially to the English media. But it was Davie Hay who had a terrific World Cup and I was very surprised when we got home and he was sold to Chelsea. I think that Jock had to sell a player and Davie became Celtic's biggest asset so he was the one to go.'*

As McPherson stated, Davie Hay was sold to Chelsea for a Scottish record fee of £250,000 within days of returning from the World Cup. The move came as a surprise to the player, having made his peace with the club following his winter dispute. He was considering signing a new contract but Celtic decided to cash in on him. Harry Hood recalls Hay's departure: *'The board at that time would actually influence big Jock on some occasions that they would need the money from the sale of a player.'*

Hay was an enormously popular player with the Celtic supporters and they were devastated to hear of his transfer. It was only eighteen months since Lou Macari had abdicated to Manchester United, and now another member of the *'Quality Street Gang'* had gone. Celtic chairman Desmond White was an accountant, and there was a feeling that he was overly keen to cash in on Celtic's star players. The fans now feared that a pattern concerning player sales was emerging at Celtic Park, but must have hoped that Hay would be the last one to depart.

Kenny beats Denis Connaghan in training at Seamill in May 1974, as Dixie Deans looks on.

Kenny lifts the ball over Dundee United's Pat Gardner, in the 1974 Scottish Cup final at Hampden. Steve Murray and Billy McNeill are looking on.

Kenny and Marina Harkins are
pictured in matching Celtic strips
in November 1974.

Kenny (9) congratulates Paul Wilson after Wilson's goal in the 1975 Scottish Cup final against Airdrie. Ronnie Glavin, Billy McNeill and Harry Hood can also be seen.

Kenny and Pat McCluskey stand in discussion against Derby County at Parkhead on 2nd August 1975.

Kenny scores the winning goal against Aberdeen at Parkhead on 9th August 1975.

Kenny hails Johannes Edvaldsson's goal against Derby on 2nd August 1975. Roddy MacDonald can also be seen.

Kenny takes on Hearts' defender, Don Murray, at Tynecastle on 13th August 1975.

Linda Paterson is pictured next to her hero in a photo shoot from 1975. Linda paid the princely sum of £1.50 for the pleasure.

Kenny salutes Johannes Edvaldsson after his goal at Parkhead against Dumbarton on 16th August 1975.

Kenny fires a cross past Des Bremner of Hibs at Parkhead on 18th October 1975.

Kenny and Marina receive a presentation from Tom Stewart of the Dublin Celtic supporters club in Dublin in January 1976.

Kenny shoots for goal against St Johnstone at Muirton Park on 17th January 1976. Ian MacDonald is the Saints player.

Caricature poster
of Kenny, bought
from street vendor at
Celtic Park in 1977.

Kenny shoots for goal against
Leeds United at Parkhead
on 11th February 1976. Keith
Parkinson is the Leeds player.

Kenny scores against Sachsenring Zwickau at Parkhead,
in the European Cup Winners Cup, on 3rd March 1976.

Kenny is reunited with his 1977 Scottish Cup final medal after
he had lost it celebrating with Celtic fans after the match.

Kenny lifts the Scottish Cup as Celtic captain at Hampden
on 7th May 1977. Celtic beat Rangers 1-0 in the final.

CHAPTER NINE
REAL DISAPPOINTMENT - 1974/1975

Scottish football did not experience any noticeable boost from Scotland's appearance in the 1974 World Cup finals. From the start of the season attendances were down. One obvious factor was that Celtic's nine year dominance in the league had resulted in a certain amount of apathy, resulting in lower crowds, even at Celtic Park.

Another factor seen to be affecting attendances was that Scottish clubs were no longer able to hold on to their star players, and were vulnerable to bids from English teams. Celtic had recently lost Davie Hay to Chelsea, and around the same period Alfie Conn (Rangers), Alex Cropley (Hibs), John Duncan (Dundee), Alex Forsyth (Partick Thistle) and Keith McRae (Motherwell) had all departed south of the border for large transfer fees.

A new *'Premier'* League of ten teams had been organised, and was due to start in season 1975-76. It was hoped that the opportunity of a place in the new set up would create some much needed competition. The clubs would do battle for one the ten places available in the new league. From a Celtic perspective however, the main incentive for the new season was the opportunity of going for a world record tenth successive league title, which would surpass Bulgarian side, CSKA Sofia, who also had nine.

Celtic's big curtain raiser for the new season saw them play Liverpool, in a richly deserved testimonial game for club captain Billy McNeill. Bill Shankly had rocked the football world by announcing his shock resignation as Liverpool boss, and he managed his beloved team for the final time. The game featured British football's two brightest stars in Kenny Dalglish and Kevin Keegan. However both men were overshadowed by their striking colleagues, as John Toshack scored for Liverpool and Paul Wilson for Celtic, in a 1-1 draw. McNeill presented all players who participated with a canteen of cutlery and he was reckoned to be £70,000 better off following his testimonial events.

....

John Monteath recalls meeting Kenny for the first time.

> In 1974 my wife's cousin was getting married to Alfie Conn and my wife and I were invited to the wedding. Walking into the reception, I could see virtually the whole Rangers team and Willie Morgan from Manchester United but there on the dance floor with Marina was my hero! I was beside myself, I was so happy and I couldn't take my eyes off him. An hour or so into it my mother in law (God bless her) came up to our table and said - 'I've just asked that Kenny Dalglish if he would mind if I took a picture of him with my son in law because you're such a big fan of his.' So I sheepishly went over to the table and there he was in conversation with the dreaded John Greig. I shuffled to Kenny's side, mumbled something to him about how great he was and my mother in law took the pic. When the pic came back from the chemist (remember those days?), there we were....me, my hero AND John Greig! But at least I got to meet Kenny.

....

Kenny may not have played as well as he had hoped in the World Cup finals but being in West Germany had greatly increased his exposure as a footballer. He was regarded as the finest player in Scotland, and in an increasingly commercial world, he appeared keen to cash in on his rising fame. Jim McGinley's father, also named Jim, ran a busy travel agency in Berkeley Street, Glasgow. He was a Celtic fan and Jim junior recalls the day when his father received some familiar visitors: *'My old man was in his office one day when (I think) Pat McCluskey, Danny McGrain and possibly Jimmy Quinn came in to book a holiday. They said they had someone outside who wanted to speak to him and they brought in a very shy Kenny. My dad was asked to be his agent and had to decline because of business commitments but he did send Kenny on to a chap called Tony Meehan who I think advised Kenny for years. Kenny said that he was now being asked to give some interviews and maybe even ghost write a column somewhere and it was suggested that he get an 'agent'. He didn't know anyone and I think it was the late John Quinn of the Evening Times who suggested he speak to my dad. Meehan was an interesting guy. As I recall he was one of the original DJ's on the old Radio Scotland Pirate ship with Richard Park and others. I believe my Dad helped him at the start of his marketing career by helping him get a job with Rothman's cigarettes - he got a similar job for a guy called Jim Trainor who went on to be a right hand man to Jack Nicklaus in America. I used to slag my dad rotten about turning down Kenny.'*

Meehan wasted to no time in launching a publicity drive to raise the profile of his two newest clients, Kenny, and Sandy Jardine of Rangers. In an interview in the Daily Record headlined *'Mr Ten Percent'*, he explained how times were changing and that footballers could be marketable commodities: *Come Christmas the athletic figures of Kenny Dalglish and Sandy Jardine (although never together!) will be pinned on thousands of bedroom walls up and down the country, alongside pop superstars Donny Osmond and David Essex. At least that's the aim of 31 year old London born Tony Meehan, who could become the next big manager in Scottish football. Not in the Jock Stein sense but as Mr Ten Per Cent (at least)...the man handling the commercial prospects of Scotland's soccer stars. World Cup men Dalglish and Jardine are the first in the stable of the impressively named International Image Consultants, part of a worldwide publicity and advertising group based in Glasgow. Until earlier this year, IIC, for which the energetic Meehan is an articulate front man, bowled along merrily coping with the marketing problems of such varied products as brandy, tartan skirts and sausages. Then came the World Cup and the SFA called in the professionals to help make the most of the multitude of side benefits to be raked in for the SFA themselves. Exactly what Tony Meehan and his staff helped coin in for the SFA via the 'Roary Super Scot' cartoon character is still to be calculated. 'Let's just say they will make a fair bit of bread,' says Tony in discreet Madison Avenue terms. 'I think they will be pleased.'*

Certainly the whole operation must have impressed Celtic star Dalglish, who was in West Germany with Scotland, and quickly came knocking at the door asking for IIC to give him similar service. He was taken on and was quickly followed by Rangers full back Sandy Jardine. 'It has to be like this because of the peculiar social set up in Scotland,' says Tony who has lived here for 12 years since his Scots father brought the family back from London. 'To present a proper marketing package suitable for Scotland, there has to be a Celtic player and a Rangers player.

We have written to dozens of companies ranging from sports goods to petrol firms offering them the promotional services of Kenny and Sandy. It's slow going. Firms in Scotland are not yet geared to this kind of promotion but things are likely to happen.' Once they do will Meehan be willing to take on more clients? 'I should think so,' he said. 'But it would be better to bring in different sports although I don't want to build an empire.' Jardine is likely soon to sign a contract endorsing a famous make of football boots, (Dalglish is already committed), and within the next few weeks the 'pop' posters will be out. But don't expect to see Kenny or Sandy hairy chested in the Gary Glitter mould. 'We have to be conscious of the image their clubs want. Whatever commitment there is must not go against club policy.'

Just how do you 'sell' a footballer? Meehan explains, 'It's a matter of presenting a package which makes potential customers feel they will be getting value for money. At our weekly meetings I stress to the players that they must be aware of what this means. If they are contacted to promote Coca-Cola then they can't be seen drinking Pepsi. And it is also vital that they present the right image. I have stressed to them that they must be out-going personalities, always presenting an impressive front.'

Kenny had been allowed a longer summer break, along with Danny McGrain, to recover from the exertions of playing at the World Cup, so he missed the start of the season. When he did return he found it difficult to get back into his stride, and for the first time since graduating from the reserves it was felt that he had lost a bit of form. Jock Stein was patient with his star man and declared in the Celtic View: *'Dalglish is a really great club man. When that boy pulls a Celtic jersey over his head he is trying all the way. I know he's not been at his best this season but only by playing him in important matches and with the backing and encouragement of our support will he come back to his best form.'*

The Celtic team in general wasn't firing on all cylinders, and they suffered a couple of bad blows in late September and early October. During the season's first Old Firm encounter at Parkhead, Kenny gave Celtic the lead, when he lashed in a shot after hesitation by the Rangers defence. This should have been the springboard for Celtic to go on and win, but two defensive lapses allowed the Ibrox men to take both points in a 2-1 win.

The Celts then faced Greek champions, Olympiakos, in the European Cup. In the first leg at home a late Paul Wilson goal saved Celtic's blushes, giving them a 1-1 draw. As an appetiser before the game, the Scotland Ladies' International side played a Scottish Ladies' select. This was the first time a women's football game had been played on a senior ground since they were given SFA recognition.

....

The Celtic View reports on Celtic's newest supporters club.

When Celtic take on Olympiakos in Greece they'll not be completely alone. For apart from the stalwarts who always follow the team in Europe they'll be cheered on by the newest Celtic supporters' club. It's the Panathinaikos Celtic supporters club - formed right in the Greek capital. Supporters of Panathinaikos - deadly rivals of Olympiakos - decided to start a club as soon as they heard draw for the first round of the European Cup. Founder member, Anastasi Maxtakis, wrote to the View last week to tell us: 'Our two clubs have so much in common, apart from playing good football. Both play in the same colours and both clubs have a similar emblem.' The one snag about the games with Olympiakos is the present state of emergency which exists in Greece. Celtic have made provisional arrangements for the game in Athens on October 2nd but if things don't improve drastically in the next week or two then Celtic will have to seek a ruling from UEFA.

Celtic View, 2nd October 1974

....

For the second leg in Athens, Olympiakos were said to be on £1,500 per man to win the tie. Olympiakos' owner, shipping magnate Nikolas Goulandris, was reckoned to have invested £500,000 in the club, which included refurbishing the Karaiskakis stadium to host the 1971 European Cup Winners' Cup final, contested by Real Madrid and Chelsea. Celtic and Olympiakos expressed concerns about the state of the pitch on the night of the game, which Jock Stein described as the worst that Celtic had experienced in Europe. By the 23rd minute Celtic were 2-0 down, and that was how the game finished. Ecstatic Greek fans celebrated by firing firecrackers in the air after each goal, actions which led to them being banned from playing at home against Anderlecht in the next round.

On 19th October Celtic at last found their true form, when Hibs came to Celtic Park and were beaten 5-0. Dixie Deans grabbed the headlines with a hat trick, but it was the overall team display which thrilled the supporters. The game at Celtic Park was the prelude to the League Cup final between the teams, which was to be played seven days later at Hampden. During the League Cup competition there had been an experimental offside line across the eighteen yard box, and FIFA delegates were to be in attendance at the final to consider its impact.

The final was played on 26th October in front of a crowd of 53,000, and Celtic turned in another vintage performance, running out winners by 6-3. It took them only 6 minutes to take the lead with an inspired goal. A Dixie Deans' flick played in Dalglish, who then beat a man on the run, and cut the ball back for Johnstone to score easily. Deans claimed another hat trick and was christened, *'The Hammer of the Hibs'*, by the newspapers. His third goal has long remained in the memory of Celtic fans, a spectacular flying header, scored when he bulleted a wayward Johnstone shot high into the net.

Kenny had a fine game, but was unusually booked in the closing seconds. He went into a tackle with fiery Hibs winger Alex Edwards and as they tussled for the ball both men swung a kick at each other. This was most unlike Kenny, who had only accumulated two bookings in his career thus far. He always had great self discipline and stated in an interview with the Celtic View: *'It's not that I don't get annoyed but I just grit my teeth. Anyway, if I did get in to bother then I would have to face two people, Mr Stein and my father, so I don't fancy that.'*

Kenny became engaged to Marina Harkins in the spring of 1974, and the wedding date was set for November. Tony Griffin remembers the surprise of bumping into the Celtic players on Kenny's stag night: *'The last time I saw Kenny was at his stag night at the White Elephant disco in 1974. We were there on a night out and in came the Celtic first team squad. As I recall, Jinky, Bobby Lennox,*

Tommy Callaghan, and Pat McCluskey were in high spirits, shoulder charging each other, and late in the evening I visited the gents loo to find Dixie Deans washing his hair in the sink! It was a good night, and big Billy McNeill stood guard at the door all night keeping a eye on everyone.'

Prior to the wedding, the Sunday Mail printed an extensive feature on the happy couple, as they posed in matching Celtic strips for a colour photograph. Headlined - *'My £250,000 Man'*, Marina discussed their relationship in detail as they prepared to move into their new home in Newton Mearns: *'The day of our wedding is also my 21st birthday. My wedding presents and birthday gifts are all mixed up. We didn't do much of the decorating ourselves, Kenny's hopeless at that sort of thing. Kenny didn't actually propose. He just asked me if I'd like to go with him to buy a ring. I don't feel at all nervous about marrying a famous footballer, so far as I'm concerned he's just the same as everyone else. On our first date Kenny took me to see a film called Million Dollar Duck and then he bought me fish and chips.'* Kenny was quoted as saying - *'We've been very lucky, especially with the house. The club has been very good to us and if it hadn't been for the help Celtic gave us we would never have been able to afford it.'*

On 26th November Kenny and Marina were married at Netherlee Church in Glasgow. Immediately after the ceremony the couple visited Marina's grandmother Elizabeth Harkins, who was in Robroyston hospital. Meanwhile over two hundred guests waited in the New Orleans reception suite in Rutherglen to toast the happy couple. The entire Celtic squad and Jock Stein were there to wish them well, with Billy McNeill having made a mad dash from London after receiving an MBE from the Queen at Buckingham Palace. She had asked Billy, *'Are you still playing for Celtic?'*

Rangers' Sandy Jardine and John Blackley of Hibs were also guests, with the wedding menu having a football theme. Kenny and Marina were *'The match of the day'* with the guests enjoying, amongst other things, cauliflower *'au Caesar'*, *'Jinky carrots au beurr'* and *'Celtic coffee'*. Queen of the South player, Jim Donald, a friend from Kenny's Glasgow United days, was best man. Bobby Murdoch's wife, Kathleen, recalls a humorous moment from Kenny's big day: *'We were fortunate to be able to attend Kenny and Marina's wedding as Bobby, who was now a Middlesbrough player, had an injury which was keeping him from playing. Bobby sometimes had weight problems during his time at Celtic and as the meal arrived I could see Jock Stein peering over to see what Bobby was eating. I caught Jock's attention and I said to him, 'It's none of your business now' and we both started laughing.'*

Stein was delighted to see Kenny settle down to married life. He believed players in stable relationships would be less likely to succumb to the temptations of various vices which could affect their form as footballers. He believed that players became better professionals with the responsibilities that came with marriage and family life.

Married life obviously suited Kenny and he gave arguably his best performance in a Celtic jersey, when Celtic played Dundee at Dens Park in December. He scored a sensational hat trick in Celtic's 6-0 win with a great individual performance, and accolades followed at every turn. In the Celtic View John McPhail stated that: *'This young man has played many fine games in a Celtic jersey but I have no hesitation in saying this was the best of them all. It was a performance to rank with the legendary displays of the heroes of the past.'*

Dundee defender Iain Phillip had played in the English first division with Crystal Palace, and he rated Kenny the best player in the UK. He remarked in the Daily Record: *'He is fast off the mark, has amazing control and bewildering body swerves. One wee moment can send you out of the park while Kenny moves in on goal.*

He is better than all the big names down south. Rodney Marsh is a bit like him in the way he takes defenders on. But Kenny has more vision than Marsh.'

Rod Stewart and the Faces were in Glasgow in December to play five nights at the Glasgow Apollo. Rod took the opportunity to travel to Dundee to support Celtic. Before kick off he caused a stir in the city, when thousands of people turned up to see him open Bruce's record shop in Reform Street. Rod was friendly with Kenny and the Celtic players, as they had dropped in on Rod after previous concerts in Glasgow. After the game, The Weekly News ran an interview with Kenny and asked him to name his top ten favourite records, which included a few of Rod's biggest hits:

1. *Maggie May - Rod Stewart*

2. *Please stay - The Crying Shames*

3. *Down at the club - The Drifters*

4. *Twistin' the night away - Rod Stewart*

5. *Your song - Elton John*

6. *You'll never walk alone - Gerry and the Pacemakers.*

7. *Mandolin wind - Rod Stewart*

8. *I can't stand to go on without you - The Drifters*

9. *Hey Jude - The Beatles*

10. *Passing time - Jimmy Johnstone*

On the terraces the Celtic fans' new song for the season was, *'It's magic you know - it's gonnae be ten in a row'*, to the tune of Pilot's hit single *'Magic'*, in anticipation of a record tenth league title win.

Celtic went into the vital Old Firm game at Ibrox on 4th January 1975 in fine spirits, and with a two point advantage over Rangers. The Ibrox side opened the scoring through Derek Johnstone, but for the rest of the half Celtic played well and created chances. Paul Wilson had an exceptional match, but when Harry Hood missed from three yards, and Kenny from eight yards, it began to look like it wasn't to be Celtic's day.

Tommy McLean made it 2-0 after 50 minutes, but even then Kenny was desperately close to scoring on a couple of occasions. When Derek Parlane made it 3-0 the Celtic fans knew it was all over. In the second half Rangers grew stronger in midfield, the first real indication that Celtic were missing the forceful presence of Davie Hay. The frustrating thing was that Celtic could easily have won this game had they taken their chances. Hay's aggression in midfield would be sorely missed until the appearance of a young Roy Aitken in 1976.

In later years Kenny would comment in the Celtic View that: *'The memory of that game keeps reappearing like a bad dream. If we had scored early on, and I missed a great chance, we would have equalised and I think gone on to win. But we can't complain, part of the trouble was bad form, part of it bad luck. Maybe after nine seasons when we had a bit of luck at the time we needed it, this was the season when it ended.'*

The Ibrox match was to be the turning point of the season. Rangers pushed on as Celtic faltered, with a home defeat to Motherwell and insipid draws against Arbroath and Dumbarton causing further damage. By the time Celtic lost 2-1 at Easter Road in late February, it was obvious that Celtic's ten in a row challenge was in tatters.

In a fine piece of prose, Ian Archer writing for the Glasgow Herald, perfectly summed up the mood of the time: *The crown lies shakily on Celtic's head. One little nudge and it will roll in one huge clatter, down the steps of the throne from which they have ruled this Scottish Kingdom these past nine years. There should be much sadness abroad in the land. Coming back by rail from the capital, looking into the deep set eyes of Celtic supporters who seemed to have fought a long campaign in the desert rather than attended a football match, you were in touch with grief. Those of us who have tugged at their shirt tails for so long and felt proud to be with them when the plane touched down at some foreign capital, to find that their fame had preceded them, found no joy at all in desperate, possibly ruinous defeat at Easter Road. This last decade has established Celtic as one of the great clubs in the world. Not as lastingly famous as the unique Real Madrid, not as individually talented or explosive as Ajax of Amsterdam. But more friendly and better loved than Inter, more attractive than any English club since the last revival of Tottenham Hotspur. They trod more new paths than any Scotsman since David Livingstone left Blantyre. So when the lights were turned up and the part finished, when it was seen that under the make up was a tired face, when all that happened on Saturday it was difficult not to cry a little, for if Celtic made their own players rich and famous, their own fans a few inches taller, mere observers a little happier, they made Scotland a good deal better. These were Saturday's thoughts, morose and made worse by the historical probability that we shall never see their like again. A part of everyone who likes his football has disappeared from his soul as, in these last few weeks, the glory of the nine years has vanished in the confusion of the tenth.*

The inevitable happened on 29th March, when Rangers clinched their first title since 1964, against Hibs at Easter Road. Following the inevitable hysteria in the Scottish media, one Celtic supporter remarked that it was, *'Not so much a league championship victory but more a relief of Mafeking.'*

The Celtic View attempted to deflect attention from Celtic's poor form by reporting that the American dare devil motor cyclist, Evel Knievel, was to visit Celtic Park in June to jump over a number of double decker buses. However, Knievel never did come to Parkhead. Ultimately, the Celtic fans were more concerned with their team's poor performances than the non-appearance of a stuntman.

One week later Kenny was given the honour of captaining Celtic for the first time, when they drew 1-1 with Morton at home. Despite their inconsistent league form, Celtic managed to fight their way to the Scottish Cup final in May, when they faced Airdrieonians at Hampden. Incredible as it may seem, several journalists predicted an Airdrie victory, given Celtic's run of poor form, and that fact that Airdrie had impressively beaten both Celtic and Rangers in the weeks leading up to the final.

Paul Wilson's mother sadly passed away just days before the final. Jock Stein left the decision of whether to play in the final to his player. The Celtic striker showed great courage by turning out, and became Celtic's hero, scoring twice in a 3-1 win. Kenny was used to getting a lift to Parkhead from Billy McNeill, and the Celtic captain had confided in him on the morning of the game that he was to retire after the final. The fans and media were oblivious to McNeill's decision until after the game, but there is no doubt the Celtic players gave their all to provide their captain with the great send off he richly deserved after seventeen years service.

....

Wilson was the goal scoring hero but Dalglish was to receive the plaudits afterwards:

> And then there was Dalglish, of the straight back, the supple legs, the wondrous touch and sure vision. He cantered through this match avoiding the tackles, spraying the play, and dribbling like a ballet dancer over the minefield of swinging legs. He was the artist of the afternoon when the picture was painted on the broadest canvas of all.

Glasgow Herald, 5th May, 1975

....

Celtic's cup final line up showed great change from their 1974 cup winning side. The team was: Latchford, McGrain and Lynch;

Murray, McNeill and McCluskey; Hood, Glavin and Dalglish; Lennox and Wilson. Latchford, Lynch, Glavin, Wilson and unused substitute, Roddy MacDonald, all won winners medals for the first time.

One week after their Scottish Cup victory, Celtic returned to Hampden to play Rangers in the Glasgow Cup final. This competition had all but died out, but much was made of the 800th anniversary of Glasgow's burgh charter, and a match between the two great Glasgow clubs was seen as a fitting way to help celebrate the event. This proved a popular idea with the fans and 82,000 tickets were sold in advance. However, foul weather limited the attendance to 70,494 on the day. Paul Wilson scored twice for Celtic in a 2-2 draw, leaving honours even.

With the club season over and the Home International fixtures looming, Alex Cameron took time to lavishly praise Kenny in his Daily Record column: *'Kenny Dalglish may soon be the most highly valued player in the land. And he will also fill the gap left by his mentor, Billy McNeill. Dalglish has confirmed in the last two cup finals involving Celtic that he is striding elegantly towards greatness, having recovered from the ache of a World Cup hangover. It is around him that the new Celtic will be built. Just as the lynchpin of the halcyon Stein era was McNeill, the career of Dalglish is now pointed in the same direction. Dalglish could be designated captain next season, a gesture which would indicate to Celtic fans that he is there for good. Opponents and team mates raved about the way Dalglish set up Celtic's second goal against Rangers. He strode past defenders like a green and white ghost with ball bearings for hips. He has the elegance of Charlton, the strength of Di Stefano and flair approaching that of Pele. I have seen all the great players of the last 25 years from Pele downwards and would rate them this way: 1-Pele; 2-Di Stefano; 3-Puskas; 4-Baxter. If Dalglish can strike his club form in internationals he will certainly be among this elite group and perhaps even top the lot. His passing is perfect and shielding the ball so naturally done that opponents find it nearly impossible to roust him off it. Sometimes his finishing is a weakness as it was in the cup final. All great players have their weaknesses, however. Dalglish's temperament is good but will improve when he overcomes a tendency to nark referees. Pietro Anastasi cost Juventus £410,000. Nobody could buy Dalglish for that now, even if Celtic dared to part with him. If Dalglish turns on his top form against England at Wembley he can establish himself as Britain's number one. Dalglish is nearly the professional player with a code of conduct no manager could fault. His worth to Celtic may be even greater than McNeill's.'*

After appearing in the draw against Wales and the win against Northern Ireland, Kenny was selected for the Scots to face England at Wembley. Before the game, England manager Don Revie stated that he regarded Kenny as the main danger to his side. However England were rampant and ran out winners by 5-1, much to the angst of the huge Scottish support in the stadium. Although the two Celts on display, Dalglish and McGrain, were regarded as Scotland's best players on the day, this was little consolation. Rangers' goalkeeper, Stewart Kennedy, had enjoyed a tremendous season at Ibrox, but the brunt of the criticism was aimed at him, and he was never chosen to play for his country again.

It should be noted that Scotland's Leeds United players were not available for selection, as they were preparing for their European Cup final match against Bayern Munich in Paris. This meant Billy Bremner, Peter Lorimer, Joe Jordan and Eddie Gray were all unavailable, which was a considerable disadvantage for Willie Ormond. Gordon McQueen was suspended for the European Cup Final and was able to play in the Wembley debacle.

Season 1974-75 had been Kenny's most difficult one to date, with a curious mixture of successes and disappointments. However, a non footballing incident was to occur in the summer of 1975 which would greatly affect Kenny, Celtic and Scottish football in general.

CHAPTER TEN
CAPTAIN FANTASTIC - 1975/1976

On 5th July 1975, Jock Stein was driving back to Glasgow from Manchester airport. Stein had been on holiday in Tony Queen's holiday villa in Minorca. Stein's wife Jean, Bob Shankly and his wife Margaret, and Tony Queen, were all passengers in his Mercedes car on the journey home. On a notorious stretch of the A74 road near Dumfries, Jock moved out to overtake a lorry. As he did so, another car driving on the wrong side of the dual carriageway came straight at Stein, resulting in a head on collision. Jock spent four weeks in Dumfries Royal infirmary, having sustained severe chest wounds, fractured ribs and injuries to his hips and feet. Newspaper photographs of the mangled Mercedes showed that Jock and his passengers had been more than fortunate to survive. Tony Queen, who had been asleep in the front passenger seat, was said to have woken up in hospital three weeks after the crash.

The Glasgow Herald reported that on 5th December 1975 at Dumfries sheriff court, 43 year old John Ballantyne was found guilty of driving recklessly and of driving whilst under the influence of alcohol. He had consumed more than twice the legal limit. He was fined £200 and was banned from driving for eighteen months, having denied the charges against him. Ballantyne was found to have been driving on the wrong side of the A74 dual carriageway, using it as a short cut, known to be taken by people in the Dumfries area.

Stein would take a long time to recuperate after the crash. Celtic directors met and announced that Sean Fallon would take over the running of the team until Stein's return, which was hoped would be in time for the start of season 1976-77. However many doubted that he would ever resume his duties as Celtic manager. Journalist Rodger Baillie was a close friend of Stein's, and he saw at first hand the injuries Jock had suffered: *'It was extremely serious. The first time I saw him after the crash was when I went to his house the day after he came home. You had to wonder if he really would come back. Before the crash Jock had been 24/7, 365 days a year, and he just wasn't as energetic afterwards.'*

Sean Fallon had major problems to contend with as interim boss at Parkhead. Billy McNeill's retiral had left a huge void and a new captain would have to be appointed. Experienced players Jimmy Johnstone and Jim Brogan had been given free transfers in the close season, and would prove difficult to replace. George Connelly walked out on Celtic again in September 1975, and this time it was to be for good. Celtic also lost popular midfielder Steve Murray, when he developed a toe problem which was to eventually end his career.

Fallon had just watched Celtic beat English champions, Derby County, in a prestigious pre-season friendly, when the club were rocked by a transfer request from Kenny Dalglish. This was the last thing Fallon needed, and the request, given the fact that Jock Stein was still in hospital, was seen as ill timed. For two weeks Celtic were at the centre of transfer drama, with rumours abounding that Dalglish was to move on.

Kenny explained his reasons for asking away to the media, having refused Celtic's new terms for the season: *'It is true I have asked for a transfer but I really don't want to leave Celtic. I love the club and I love the fans who have been tremendous to me. I feel I have been forced into this. If things don't work out then I'm afraid I'll have to leave.*

That's the way it is but I have no alternative after the signing talks I have had.'

Dalglish was rated in the £300,000 bracket and there would be no shortage of suitors for his signature. On 9th August he turned in a terrific performance, scoring an impressive goal against Aberdeen in Celtic's 1-0 win. Everton, Manchester United and Leeds United all had representatives in the Parkhead stand that day, and were said to be greatly interested in Celtic's star man.

As an established internationalist Kenny would have been very aware of how much his English based counterparts were earning. Tony Meehan's marketing work would also have reinforced the fact that he was the top rated player in the Scottish game. Meehan, although not Kenny's formal agent, had inside knowledge of how a footballer such as Dalglish should be rewarded.

It may have been coincidence, but Sandy Jardine, also represented by Meehan, had tried the same thing at Ibrox, resulting in a considerable wage rise for the Rangers full back. Celtic's terms for the new season had not been to Kenny's satisfaction, prompting the transfer request. His decision met with mixed reviews.

In the Sunday Mail Allan Herron launched a withering attack on the timing of his demands in an article headlined - ***Kenny Dalglish - Football's Oliver Twist***: *'Kenny Dalglish, the footballer who has everything the schoolboy dreams about, suddenly holds out his hand in the best Oliver Twist tradition and asks for more. The timing of his request bears no resemblance to his treatment of a ball on the field. His manager Jock Stein is recovering from a serious car accident, the team captain has retired and the football industry, like any other, is toiling under economic pressure. But Kenny, at the age of 24 years, married to a pretty wife with a home of his own and a quality car, wants more. He is the golden boy of Scottish football, having made 27 successive appearances under Willie Ormond, and having cashed in to the hilt as an international player from the Celtic stable. He is perhaps* *the best paid player in Scottish football. He served an apprenticeship with the men who brought the European Cup back to Scotland but he cannot come to terms with the club that made him. I'm all for players making the most from their short term careers but there are occasions when they push too hard, Dalglish should think again. He has it made at Parkhead and his future is secure there. The grass may look greener in England where players talk money in telephone numbers and loyalty is almost non-existent. Celtic chairman, Desmond White, will make a statement on his number one player in the next few days. It gives Kenny Dalglish some thinking time. Maybe he'll just struggle by on what Celtic pay him after all...'*

In the Daily Record, Alex Cameron struck a more conciliatory tone: *'Dalglish is not in the usual run of dissatisfied men for he is not out of love with Celtic or anyone connected with it. He wants more money but there is nothing original or disloyal about this. Celtic, without Dalglish, look fairly ordinary but I am sure he is not naive enough to feel indispensible. Dalglish is balanced as if he trained on a trampoline and he runs for ninety like a man who hopes to win a marathon. Frankly, his talent should not be lost to Scottish fans, even if there are ten times more fans in England. The football brain-drain down south has to be blocked or the new Premier League will simply be training ground for England.'*

The most serious interest in Dalglish came from Leeds United, who were reported to have offered £240,000, plus Scotland captain Billy Bremner, in part exchange. Bremner was a Scotland legend but at 32, was considered to be too old. Celtic also appeared to have been making moves behind the scenes to spend any fee they might receive for Kenny, as Harry Hood recalls hearing about: *'In 1975 Leeds United bid £240,000 for Kenny, which was a record at that time. Celtic wanted to do a deal with Jim McLean at Dundee United for David Narey and Andy Gray. United wanted over £100,000. Celtic thought this was too much money, and bid about £80,000 for the pair, which they were never likely to get.'*

Behind the scenes Sean Fallon was able to perform an element of manoeuvring between Dalglish and the Celtic board. As caretaker manager Sean was responsible for choosing a new captain. In pre-season games Bobby Lennox, as Celtic's most experienced player, had captained the side. However this was not to be a long term solution. With the Celtic board reluctant to give in to any wage demands, Fallon suggested that Kenny should be made captain, in the knowledge that he would be due extra money for the responsibilities of the captaincy, therefore allowing Celtic to save face. This seemed the best decision to resolve a difficult situation.

On 19th August Celtic announced that Kenny had signed a new two year contract with the club. Chairman Desmond White said to the press: *'We have come to agreement with Kenny Dalglish and he is staying with Celtic. Hopefully he will be here for the rest if his career.'*

The Celtic board deserved credit for sorting out a difficult situation. They had agreed to a wage increase to keep Kenny, despite announcing losses of £19,000 for the financial year. However, it is worth noting that Chelsea reportedly still owed the club £80,000 from the transfer of David Hay.

A happy Kenny confirmed he was staying at Celtic, when he spoke to the Daily Record at his Newton Mearns home: *'Things are now settled. I had a problem about conditions but that was all cleared up in the talks with the club. I can't say how happy I am. I didn't want to leave Celtic and I meant it. They are the greatest club in the world. The Celtic fans have always been good to me. They were even better during this trouble. Their encouragement helped me on the field and convinced me that I didn't want to play anywhere else.'* The new deal was now reckoned to be worth £200 a week for Dalglish, and it was left to the astute Fallon to comment - *'It's better to have money on the park than money in the bank.'*

The Celtic View was inundated with letters from happy fans saying how pleased they were that their best player was staying, and had been made club captain. On 20th August Kenny led the Celts out at Parkhead to play Hearts, and received a fantastic reception. The fans belted out the chant - *'Super Ke-enny, super Ke-enny, super Kenny Dalglish! Super Kenny Dalglish!'* to the catchy tune of the Wombles latest chart hit, *'Super Womble'*. The fans also sang their version of Rod Stewart's hugely successful song, *'Sailing'*, which became a number one chart hit in August 1975. The supporters raised their scarves aloft as they sang it, and for a couple of seasons this song replaced *'You'll Never Walk Alone'* in the Celtic fans' repertoire.

As Celtic captain, Kenny had an even higher profile for Tony Meehan to work with, as the Daily Mail's Brian Scott was to discover in late August: *Kenny Dalglish, Celtic and Scotland's £200 per week footballer, went on sale yesterday. For an undisclosed fee, Dalglish posed with hundreds of fans who streamed to his eight hour photographic session in a shop-cum-studio at the city's Barrowland Market. They paid £1.50 for the privilege of being snapped in colour with the snappiest player in the country. And others who were too shy to say 'cheese' with Kenny were allowed to watch from a gallery for 30p. All the while a steady trade was done in such items as Kenny Dalglish T-shirts with Dalglish collecting the royalties. The money spinning idea came from a Glasgow businessman and was instantly welcomed in the pennywise world of Soccer. Dalglish found it rewarding in more ways than one. 'Most of the folk who have come here have been Celtic fans and it's been good to talk to them.' Can he see the time when he might be a football millionaire? He joked: 'I'll need to win the pools to do that.' Similar photographic sessions with other personalities are planned for future Sundays so look out for the Rangers' international Sandy Jardine being brought into the picture. He and Dalglish are both managed by Glasgow commercial agent, Tony Meehan, who said: 'The idea of having Kenny here was put to me, and Kenny agreed to it. He never undertakes anything which is against the wishes of the club and we seek their permission for every venture.' The camera began clicking at 10am and one of the first fans who watched the birdie with Kenny was Brian McCrory from Kilmarnock. He said: 'I have travelled up to Glasgow especially for this. I'm a great Celtic fan and the idea of getting my photo taken with Kenny really appealed to me. After all, he's worth £300,000.' That is the transfer market value of course, with the player's contract believed to be worth £10,000 a year. Meehan said: 'Kenny can become a rich man. How rich I cannot say. It depends on what business comes in but things are going well at the moment.' Dalglish and Jardine have been involved in numerous money making schemes including beer advertisements for commercial radio. In the offing for both, who are shortly to be the subjects of a TV documentary, are contracts for footballs and a special supporters' shirt, while Kenny is to go it alone at the Glasgow Motor show on behalf of an Italian car company.*

Shortly after this appearance, Dalglish and Jardine posed alongside new footballs bearing their names, green and white for Kenny and blue and white for Sandy. Rangers had just won the first Old Firm game at Ibrox by 2-1, with Kenny scoring Celtic's goal. This game had been another occasion when Celtic missed several opportunities to score. The new Premier League set up would see teams face each other four times in the course of a season, so there would be plenty of opportunities for Celtic to exact revenge.

One week later Jock Stein made a welcome visit to Parkhead to witness Celtic's 4-0 win over Dundee. Stein was given a standing ovation from the patrons of the main stand, although it was said that he was a long way off from returning as Celtic manager.

In September 1975, the Weekly News produced a quaint tribute to Celtic's new captain. In Scots' dialect, a poem was printed to be sung to the popular tune of Galway Bay, entitled - *Kenny, The Nijinsky of Celtic Park.*

If ye walk oot London Road ayond the Barras
Ye'll come upon a street called 'Kerrydale'
And if ye leftwards glance ye'll quickly notice
The back o' Celtic's grandstand without fail

Noo if there should be a hame gemme oan ye'll hear, folks
An awfy din - na modicum o' wheesh
And then you can bet the fans are acclaimin'
Their golden boy, their maestro - KEN DALGLISH!

Wi' his crony Sandy Jardine o' the Rangers
Kennys made a record o' his dulcet tones
But ah don't think it'll cause much apprehension
Tae Humperdinck or his big pal Tom Jones!

Naw, it's oan the fitba' fiel' that Kenny dazzles
He's lissom, agile, craftyn - never coarse
And sae graceful that he minds me o' Nijinsky
Coorse, ah mean thae ballet dancer no' the hoarse!

Kenny's commercial activities were on the increase, and in October the popular Shoot magazine announced Kenny as their new signing as a fortnightly columnist. Shoot was a UK wide publication, giving Kenny even greater exposure. Journalist, Chick Young, recalls how lucrative a business this was for Kenny: *'I was to ghost write his columns at different times for Shoot magazine and the Evening Times newspaper and I would reckon at that time he was getting as much from his media work as he was from Celtic. Tony Meehan was a ahead of his time in terms of the marketing he was doing at that time although things didn't always come off. I went to a 'worst record' dinner party where you were to bring the worst record you've ever heard and I took along 'Each Saturday' by Kenny and Sandy Jardine. It was that bad.'*

Kenny's reign as Celtic's captain started promisingly, with the Celts top of the league and doing well in the European Cup Winners'

Cup. However, the first big test was to end in disappointment in late October, when Rangers beat Celtic 1-0 at Hampden, in the League Cup final. Celtic officials were angered by Tom Forsyth's rough tackles on Kenny, which were allowed to go unchecked by referee Bill Anderson. Forsyth was already on a booking when he badly fouled Danny McGrain, and he was fortunate not to be ordered off. Sean Fallon was mystified as to Anderson's selection as the match official: *'There are seven FIFA ranked refs but not one was given the final. All the best refs were ignored. It seems a strange decision when a FIFA listed ref is not given such a top game'.*

On 5th November Kenny inspired the Celts to a 3-1 win at Parkhead against Boavista of Portugal. This result sent Celtic through to the quarter finals, on a 3-1 aggregate scoreline, although they had walked a tight rope before Kenny's exquisite pass allowed Dixie Deans to score Celtic's third, late in the game.

Later in November the Celtic Supporters' Association held a function in Glasgow's City Halls to commemorate the record achievement of winning nine league titles in a row. A commemorative flag was handed over to the club by the association, and Frank McElhone MP, the secretary of state and minster of sport for Scotland, was a guest speaker. McElhone recalled: *'I remember well the less successful years at Parkhead and this is where we have the advantage over the younger generation. There is rich caviar now but those of us who have seen the other days appreciate there were times when the jam was spread pretty thin. However, these times are still worth remembering. There were brilliant players, and I recall the wonderful artistry of Charlie Tully and the match winning ability of Jimmy Delaney. And this is matched today by the skill of your present captain, Kenny Dalglish.'*

Shortly after this event Celtic travelled down to Somerset Park to face Ayr United in a difficult midweek match. Ayr had just defeated Rangers 3-0 and were on an impressive run of form. Supporters at this game witnessed another of Kenny's greatest goals, when he ran from half way, played a one-two with Paul Wilson, and lashed a shot high into the net from outside the area. Celtic were unstoppable and ran out 7-2 winners. Chick Young recalls why he missed Kenny's great effort: *'I wrote the match report that night at Somerset Park but never saw Kenny's goal. I was working for a newspaper and the phone booth was under the stand. Every fifteen minutes I had to report my copy to the office and each time I went away I missed one or two goals. It took the other journalists to describe to me how good a goal it was. There were nine goals that night and I think I must have missed five of them.'*

Three days after their scintillating win in Ayrshire, Celtic frustrated their supporters by losing 2-0 at home to Motherwell. Inconsistency had crept into their play, something that was to curse them all season. As captain, Kenny remarked in the Celtic View at how difficult things were for his team in the new, more competitive, Premier League: *'The Lisbon Lions were a marvellous team, one of the greatest sides Scotland has ever produced. But times have changed. Scottish teams are now a lot better organised than they were ten years ago. A lot of managers are putting a lot of thought into it.'*

....

The Celtic View reveals how some of the players spend their leisure time.

I play golf though not as well as I would like. Kenny Dalglish and I are foursome partners and we are undefeated champions of Parkhead. There have been a lot of hints about cutting our handicaps (I'm off 20 and Kenny's off 15). We'll resist that of course. The match prize is always golf balls...and neither Kenny or I have had to buy any for some time.

Pat McCluskey interview, Celtic View 1976

....

In early 1976 Kenny was selected as player of the year by the Dublin Celtic Supporters Association. Kenny and Marina travelled to Dublin to receive the award, and Aer Lingus offered a two day package trip for fans for £38.50, sold through Tony Meehan Enterprises. The Dublin club chairman Tom Stewart presented Kenny with a silver coffee set, and Marina with an Irish linen table cloth. Kenny and Marina were new parents, following the birth of daughter Kelly in September.

In late January Celtic suffered a major blow when they crashed out of the Scottish Cup against Motherwell at Fir Park. Celtic were leading 2-0 at half time, by virtue of an Andy Lynch goal and a blistering twenty five yard free kick from Kenny, which had gone in like a rocket. In the second half Motherwell exposed Celtic's defensive frailties, with the striking pair of Bobby Graham and Willie Pettigrew doing most of the damage. The Steelmen pulled off a superb comeback, winning 3-2. In the aftermath Sean Fallon was said to have been keen to sign Partick Thistle's cultured defender, Alan Hansen, to bolster the Celtic defence. However Jock Stein, convalescing at home, was said to have vetoed any move for Hansen.

Leeds United visited Celtic Park in February for a challenge match, as Celtic prepared for their European Cup Winners' Cup quarter final clash, to be played against Sachsenring Zwickau of East Germany. Although Leeds won the friendly 3-1, Celtic were impressive. However Leeds manager Jimmy Armfield only had eyes for one man: *'Kenny Dalglish is a truly great player. He is one of the few who can make something out of nothing. Twice tonight he proved that by getting in shots from positions that just weren't on for anyone except an exceptionally talented player.'*

Sachsenring Zwickau were very much an unknown quality, although their captain Jurgen Croy had been rated one of the best goalkeepers during the 1974 World Cup finals. The East Germans had beaten Panathinaikos and Fiorentina in earlier rounds of the competition, and had gained a reputation for playing a defensive style of football. On 3rd March Fallon surprised many with his team selection, naming 17 year old Roy Aitken, at centre half, for what would be Aitken's third full Celtic appearance. After 24 minutes Celtic were awarded a penalty when Dalglish was fouled in the area, but the giant Croy saved the shot from Bobby Lennox. Just before half time Kenny gave Celtic the lead, and in the second half Celtic hammered away at the Sachsenring goal, but without success. Celtic's dominance was such that they had twenty one corners to Sachsenring's one, but in the last minute Ludwig Blank eluded young Aitken on the half way line, and ran on to score and equalise. The East German's turned cartwheels on the turf at full time at achieving such an unexpected result. Striker, Blank, was a headline writer's dream - *'Celts draw a Blank!'*

The second leg was to be played on St Patrick's day, which the Celtic fans hoped was a good omen. STV were showing the match live on television in the afternoon, and workers and school children hoped for time off to watch the Celts in action. Deans and Lennox were missing due to a flu epidemic which was sweeping the country. This resulted in Fallon having to play Roddy MacDonald as a makeshift striker. Blank gave Zwickau an early lead in 3 minutes, after which they defended stoutly, and Celtic were unable to break them down. In the 57th minute Celtic missed their best chance, when a powerful Glavin shot was parried by Croy, only for MacDonald to lose his footing with the empty goal gaping. There was controversy with only 4 minutes remaining. MacDonald headed in a Hood corner but the referee wrongly blew for an infringement, and the last chance was gone.

The defeat in Europe left Celtic with just the league to compete for. With seven games remaining, Celtic topped the table by a one point margin, but a 3-2 defeat at Tannadice on 10th April allowed Rangers to move in front. After this Celtic inexplicably capitulated, drawing two and losing three of their remaining six fixtures, allowing Rangers to take the title in comfortable fashion. Kenny had played a true captain's role during Celtic's league campaign. Since 3rd

January he had scored 17 league goals, an average of more than a goal a game, a truly magnificent achievement. However by 1976 it was felt that Celtic had become too reliant on Dalglish's talents, and a common phrase used by supporters at that time was - *'Dalglish carries the team on his back.'*

Sean Fallon made no excuses for Celtic's league failure, but there were certainly mitigating circumstances. Before a ball was kicked Celtic had lost Jock Stein. The experienced pair of George Connelly and Steve Murray were then both lost to Celtic, Connelly as a result of personal problems, and Murray through a cruel injury. In the spring, Fallon attempted to strengthen his team, bringing Scottish internationalists John Doyle and Jimmy Smith to Parkhead, in a bid to boost Celtic's title bid. Doyle signed for a record Celtic fee of £90,000, but was injured on his debut and missed most of the league run in. Smith had troublesome injury problems from his time at Newcastle United, and unfortunately was deemed not fit enough to risk signing. He sadly retired from football shortly afterwards.

The season was rounded off with the traditional Home Internationals, with Scotland's three fixtures all being played at Hampden. Kenny and Danny McGrain were named in the Scotland squad. Kenny had endured a torrid time from some fans during Scotland's home match against Switzerland in April. The Evening Times headline summed matters up - **Fans Attack On Dalglish Was Just Plain Sick** - and they reported: *'Some nutcases cheered when Kenny Dalglish was substituted. The Celtic captain, replaced by Des Bremner, didn't play well. The fact he took stick every time he passed a ball to his Celtic team mate Danny McGrain didn't help his case.'*

Hugh MacDonald was in attendance and recalls his feelings from that time: *'I remember being at Hampden and hearing him being booed. A lot of Celtic fans I knew wouldn't go to see Scotland in view of this. It was heart breaking to hear it, although it wasn't unusual for Celtic players to be on the end of such behaviour. Scotland players were not on the same wave length as Kenny and did not have the speed of thought or technique that he had.'*

Jeanette McCulloch recalls similar sentiments being expressed towards Kenny from members of her own family: *'My first team was actually Hibs because I loved the colours. Then in the early 1970's the Sunday Mail started colour printing and I cut out the football photos. Celtic were rampant so I became a Tim! Dalglish was magnificent, my first ever scarf was a Kenny Dalglish one. My Kilmarnock supporting dad, whilst admiring Kenny's obvious talents, used to berate him in a Scotland shirt, always muttering 'bloody rubbish.' I used to love informing him, 'Hey, bloody rubbish has just scored...again!'*

Dalglish was typically diplomatic with the press after the Swiss game, commenting that - *'They can shout what they want. Anyway, I've heard them chanting my name in praise before.'*

Scotland's opening game was against Wales and the media reported that if Kenny played he would equal George Young's record of thirty four consecutive appearances for Scotland. When the team line up was announced Kenny was on the bench, and he stayed there for the duration of the game. Afterwards there was condemnation of his non-appearance by Celtic officials, but more especially from Celtic supporters. Young was a former Rangers captain, and the feeling was that a decision had been taken to prevent a Celtic player equalling a Rangers player's record.

No one had the courtesy to explain to Dalglish why he was on the bench after thirty four successive appearances, and the feeling was that Willie Ormond had bowed to pressure from those above him. In any other country Dalglish's selection would have been automatic, to create publicity and boost the attendance, with a small presentation being deemed appropriate to mark the occasion. Frankly, Kenny deserved better treatment. He had given his all for Scotland, faithfully turning up to play in the low key friendly games which Anglo-Scots players were notorious for missing. The irony is that after this match Kenny went on another long run of appearances, eventually breaking Young's record in March 1980, in a game against Portugal. However by this time he was a Liverpool player. Had he played against Wales in 1976, Kenny would have broken the world record of seventy successive international appearances held by England's Billy Wright.

In the next game against Northern Ireland Kenny was recalled, and scored in a 3-0 victory, setting up a championship decider against England. The English came north with the usual hype, and a string of big name players in Roy McFarland, Colin Todd, Kevin Keegan, Gerry Francis and Mike Channon. Much was made of Alan Rough's appearance in goals for Scotland, given that he played for lowly Partick Thistle, who were in Scottish football's second tier at the time. Although England took the lead with a Channon header, the Scots grew stronger as the game went on. Don Masson equalised, then on the stroke of half time there was huge controversy. Kenny went on a great run from deep, beating two players, and as England goalkeeper Ray Clemence threw himself at Dalglish's feet, he sent him crashing to the turf. The home fans screamed in unison for a penalty, but referee Karoly Palotai enraged the Scots by copping out and blowing for half time.

In the second half Scotland were the superior side, and took the lead with as memorable a goal as the old stadium ever witnessed. Joe Jordan crossed from the left to find Kenny in the English area. Mick Mills was blocking the road to goal but Kenny managed to get his shot away. It wasn't a powerful effort, but as Ray Clemence knelt down to gather the ball he inexplicably let it slip through his legs, and it slowly rolled into the net. Hampden exploded and Kenny ran off to receive the acclaim of the Scottish support. Scottish goalkeeping against England had long been criticised, but in this match one of the most renowned English keepers made one of the worst blunders ever witnessed in encounters between the two countries.

The best move of the game came late on, when the Celtic pairing of Dalglish and McGrain combined delightfully to send the full back in on goal, but Danny could only shoot tamely at Clemence from fifteen yards. Scotland ran out 2-1 winners and the players celebrated joyfully after the match, as they paraded the Home International trophy in front of the Hampden crowd.

Forty eight hours after his endeavours at Hampden, Kenny lined up for Celtic against Manchester United in a joint testimonial game for Jimmy Johnstone and Bobby Lennox. Dalglish continued his sparkling form, with a tremendous hat trick in a 4-0 victory. The match was played in front of 48,000 appreciative fans who turned out for two of Celtic's most revered players. Chelsea allowed Davie Hay to play for Celtic on the night. He gave a typically determined performance and the Celtic fans sang, *'We want Hay'*, in appreciation. The fans were keen for Hay to return to Celtic, as there had been rumours that Chelsea were unable to pay Celtic the remainder of Hay's transfer fee, but nothing materialised.

Jimmy Johnstone was then plying his trade in England with Sheffield United, and he embarked on one last emotional lap of honour as the fans roared their approval. In an interview with the Sunday Mail the wee man gave a glowing tribute to his old Celtic team mate: *If any youngster wants to model himself on a player, then Kenny Dalglish is the man. He is undoubtedly one of the modern day greats and his attitude was always right, on and off the park. He had fantastic close control and had the ability to turn on a sixpence. Kenny was also very courageous, a point which is often ignored when people talk about him. He took a lot of hefty knocks but jumped up and kept on playing. I've seen times when his leg was strapped up heavily but he still wanted to play. He had a great appetite for football and that made him an extraordinary professional in my book.*

CHAPTER ELEVEN
THE LAST HURRAH - 1976/77

Jock Stein returned to the helm at Celtic Park during the summer of 1976. Around this time Celtic revealed some changes to the backroom staff at the club. The Celtic scouting system within Scotland was totally overhauled and Sean Fallon was appointed as head of youth development. However, the biggest surprise was that Fallon was replaced as Stein's assistant manager by former Partick Thistle manager, Davie McParland. This was a huge shock to everyone concerned, and represented a demotion for Fallon. This was difficult to comprehend, given that Sean had faithfully held the reins during Stein's absence. Celtic had admittedly failed to win a trophy during season 1975-76 but Fallon, as ever, had given his all to the Celtic cause.

Jock Stein had enjoyed a close working relationship with previous Celtic chairman, Sir Robert Kelly. However this relationship had not been replicated with his successor, Desmond White. Chairmen sometimes appear envious of the popularity that managers can enjoy with the fans and the media, and Stein was still the major figure within Scottish football. It appeared that after Stein's absence White may have been keen to dilute his power at the club. Appointing McParland was one way of doing this. McParland had a fairly ordinary record as a manager. He guided Partick Thistle to the League Cup in 1971, but at the time of his Celtic appointment he had been coaching the amateurs of Queens Park in the second division. Stein and Fallon put on a united public front, but their relationship was never to be the same. In later years Sean would admit he had been badly hurt when his influence within the club was reduced.

There was concern during the summer when Kenny had an operation on his ankle. He was thought to have damaged it as far back as the Boavista game in November, and had bravely played on until the end of the season. A family holiday in Spain gave sufficient time for the ankle to heal, and in an interview for 'Playing for Celtic No 8', Kenny was eagerly anticipating the challenge of the new campaign: 'I've heard it said we used to pick up cups so often that it was almost taken for granted. I've never accepted that but this will make us realise all the more that it's a habit we want to get back into as soon as possible. No one has a divine right to go out and win. We've all got to work for it and we're prepared to do that.'

....

The Celtic View reports on pre-match preparations ahead of the League Cup tie against Arbroath.

Celtic players made quite a splash last week - off the field. During their overnight stay in Carnoustie players and officials all cooled off with a refreshing dip in the sea. Manager Stein decided to travel north early to give the players a break and avoid Saturday morning travelling snags. Obviously his plans paid off.

Celtic View 25th August 1976, following Celtic's 5-0 win at Arbroath

....

A number of changes to the playing personnel were also evident at the start of the season. Fine servants Dixie Deans, Harry Hood and Tommy Callaghan were moved on to allow the youthful talents of Roy Aitken, Tommy Burns and George McCluskey to step up from reserve football. The early results were promising.

Celtic impressively beat Penarol in a Parkhead friendly. Kenny then grabbed the headlines by scoring with a spectacular volley, the only goal of the game in a League Cup tie at Tannadice on 14th August. This encouraging start was followed by disappointment, when Celtic lost 3-1 to Rangers in the Glasgow Cup final. The Ibrox club once again cruelly exposed Celtic's defensive failings.

Following this defeat Stein took action to remedy his team's defensive weaknesses, when he became aware that Pat Stanton was in dispute with Hibs. Stanton was one of most respected players in Scottish football, and in a shock move Hibs manager Eddie Turnbull allowed him to move to Celtic in exchange for Jackie McNamara. Stanton tells of how Stein informed him what he required: *'I was meant to be playing against Hearts reserves at Tynecastle when Eddie Turnbull phoned. He had never called me in his life so I knew something was up. He said I have Mr Stein here and he put Jock on the phone. He asked me if I'd like to play for Celtic and I met him at the Barnton hotel and signed for Celtic. Jock told me Celtic were losing too many silly goals. The problem was that when Celtic were attacking the defenders weren't paying attention and were going to sleep, so my job was to prevent this. I hardly went over the half way line all season.'*

There was mutual respect between Stanton and the Celtic players. Pat was regarded as one of the finest footballers in the country, and he in turn greatly admired Celtic's achievements under Stein. Stanton made his debut on the opening day of the season, in the heat of an Old Firm clash at Parkhead. Celtic were 2-0 down but staged a rousing comeback to draw level. Paul Wilson scored twice, the second goal being a spectacular effort, to save the day.

Having taken steps to solve Celtic's defensive problems, Stein now looked to add some strength to the attack. In mid September he signed Partick Thistle's highly rated striker, Joe Craig, for £60,000. Craig was working as a part time mechanic when he was told to report to Firhill to discuss a possible transfer. Thistle manager

Bertie Auld confirmed by telephone that one of Glasgow's big two clubs had expressed interest, but wouldn't divulge which one. Craig worked it out for himself on the journey to Maryhill that it was likely to be Celtic. He realised that Rangers already had Derek Johnstone and Derek Parlane as strikers, and therefore it would be unlikely he would be moving to Ibrox.

The biggest disappointment of the season came on the European front. In the UEFA cup Celtic were drawn against the Polish outfit, Wisla Krakow. They had a strong side, including five players from the Polish World Cup squad of 1974 - Szymanowski, Musial, Kapka, Kmiecik and Kusto. They were seen as stiff competition for a first round tie, and so it was to prove.

At Parkhead Celtic started strongly, hitting the woodwork twice before Roddy MacDonald gave them the lead. There was a large contingent of Polish fans in the main stand. They were mainly expatriates, and they waved Polish flags whilst noisily chanting *'Veesla... Veesla!'* After half time Wisla looked dangerous, and they deservedly equalised. Bobby Lennox then blundered by sending a pass back straight to Wrobel, who gave Wisla the lead. It was left to Dalglish to keep Celtic in the tie through a very late equaliser. In the second leg Celtic looked composed in the first half, and created the best chance when Paul Wilson's shot struck the Wisla 'keeper and rebounded off a post. However, in the second half Celtic buckled under pressure, and Wisla ran out 2-0 winners on the night, sending the Celts out of the competition.

....

The Celtic View reports on the trip to Poland.

The hospitality programme laid on for Celtic officials during their UEFA cup trip to Poland included lunch 500 feet down a salt mine. Of course they've had all the inevitable 'cracks' about the visit, but when they supply the details, salt mine life in Krakow sounds positively alluring. The mine, of course, is a tourist attraction. There is a museum on the first two levels, which also contains a church with the religious figures and chandeliers fashioned from salt. The underground luncheon was a lavish buffet affair but the Glasgow guests of the Wisla club found it was just a starter for there followed the usual luncheon of soup, fish, meat and sweet! Neilly Mochan had thoughts of having the Celtic officials out for training the next day. The switch of the team's headquarters from a Krakow city centre hotel to a president's mansion on the outskirts of the city gave the players a flavour of gracious living. A chef was specially installed for their stay and every meal was rated 'marvellous.' The Wisla club saw their guests had privacy. A couple of policemen with guard dogs watched over the main doorway.

Celtic View, 6th October 1976

....

Stein's new team was still at the formation stage, and Ian Archer in the Glasgow Herald observed how times had changed at Celtic Park: *'Celtic is now a team acquired rather than a team reared. Latchford, Lynch, Stanton, Glavin Craig and Doyle have all been bought for an investment of over £300,000. That, together with good leadership, should make money talk but it will take time. From the positive look of the team, Jock Stein still intends to trade goals, an attitude which can only stir the fans'.*

On 20th October Dundee United came to Celtic Park as the early season pace setters. Celtic were still finding their feet in the league, but this was the night when everything clicked into place. Celtic romped to a 5-1 victory, with all areas of the team impressing. The defence, with Stanton guiding Roddy MacDonald, looked solid. Roy Aitken had been placed in midfield as an aggressive ball winner, allowing Ronnie Glavin to move further forward in search of goals. Glavin scored a spectacular hat trick, combining well with new striker, Joe Craig, a colleague from his Partick Thistle days. In the new set up Kenny was expected to shuttle between midfield and attack which suited him: *'I did move up occasionally but most of the season I was just behind the strikers and coming through, that's what I really like best.'*

October was to prove a good month for Celtic, with Kenny Dalglish very much to the fore. He netted nine goals and produced two match winning displays in highly important games. In the League Cup semi final against Hearts, Celtic narrowly won 2-1, courtesy of two Dalglish goals. The first was a tremendous header and the second a coolly converted penalty. On the second last day of the month Motherwell came to Parkhead full of confidence, following a 3-1 win over Rangers at Fir Park. Motherwell had become somewhat of a bogey team for Celtic, with their highly rated striker Willie Pettigrew doing most of the damage. However this time the Celts were victorious and Kenny grabbed the headlines with another two tremendous goals. The first was a glorious rising shot from outside the area, and the second a crisp, early shot which took Motherwell 'keeper, Stuart Rennie, by surprise.

The League Cup final on 6th November saw Celtic come up against Ally MacLeod's rejuvenated Aberdeen side. MacLeod had made a number of impressive signings, with Stuart Kennedy, Dom Sullivan and Joe Harper all making a huge impression. The Dons thrashed Rangers 5-1 at Hampden in the semi final, giving them great confidence for the final. A crowd of 69,707 fans turned out at Hampden on a wet, murky day and were rewarded with a game of high drama. Kenny gave Celtic the lead from the penalty spot in the 12th minute, after Drew Jarvie fouled him in the area. Jarvie then equalised for Aberdeen before half time. In the second half Celtic created a series of outstanding chances to win the cup with Wilson, Doyle and McGrain all having great opportunities to score. The game went to extra time, and after only 2 minutes of the extra period Davie Robb gave the Dons the lead. Even then

Celtic had opportunities, the best falling to Bobby Lennox with 5 minutes remaining, only for him to shoot just wide. Ally MacLeod and his Aberdeen players celebrated joyfully on the Hampden turf. Aberdeen's open top bus tour of the city the next day was shown live on STV's *'Scotsport'*.

On 17th November Kenny was on World Cup duty again, when Scotland faced Wales in a qualifier at Hampden Park. This was a must win game for the Scots as they had lost their opening fixture against Czechoslovakia in Prague a month earlier. Wales were stiff opposition but one goal gave Scotland victory on the night, and it had *'made at Celtic'* stamped all over it. Danny McGrain went on a terrific overlap on the right flank, beating two Welsh defenders. From his low cross Kenny delicately flicked the ball goalwards, and Welsh defender Ian Evans inadvertently helped it into the net.

The goal was given as an Evans own goal, but in the modern game Dalglish would have been given the credit for it, as the ball was heading goalwards before it struck the unfortunate Welshman. At the end of his international career in 1986 Kenny was level with Denis Law, as Scotland's record scorer. They had 30 goals each. Had he been awarded this one, he would have finished in front of Law with 31 goals for his country.

Celtic were left to rue the fact that Pat Stanton and Joe Craig had been ineligible to play in the League Cup final. It was felt that they would have made a difference at both ends of the park. Their return to the team bolstered Celtic, who then embarked on a long unbeaten league run. On 20th November Celtic found themselves 3-1 down at Tynecastle, as Hearts' Willie Gibson became one of a select band of players to score a hat trick against the Celts. In the second half Celtic came back in spectacular style. The brilliance of Dalglish and McGrain had been Celtic's driving force, and Kenny scored the equaliser when he calmly fired his shot past two Hearts' defenders on the goal line. In the 87th minute Ronnie Glavin grabbed a terrific winner to make it 4-3 for Celtic, in what was described as the game of the season.

....

The main media attention was reserved for Dalglish and McGrain:

'Celtic must thank their skipper and international star, Kenny Dalglish, who was the most skilful player afield and matched his silky touches with a never say die attitude. He scored the all important equaliser and had a hand in the other three goals.... McGrain is arguably the best player, in any position, in the British Isles at the moment.'

Sunday Express, 21 November 1976

....

Hugh Keevins was in Edinburgh that day and his recalls Kenny's contribution: *'That afternoon at Tynecastle, he won the match almost on his own. It finished 4-3 and he was just sensational. You got the feeling that as long as he was in the team then Celtic would be okay.'*

There was another major factor in Celtic's fine win as Joe Craig remembers: *'The turning point for the whole season was the Tynecastle game. At half time we were sitting thinking how can we be losing, we had played so well. Mr Stein told us to keep playing the way we were and we would win. The main point is that when we went back out and looked at the old cow shed where the Celtic supporters were standing, they all had their scarves up, about ten thousand of them, roaring out Rod Stewart's 'We are sailing'. The noise was unbelievable and I have no doubt in my mind that those fans won us the game that day.'*

Craig was becoming a firm favourite with the Celtic supporters, and he confirmed his popularity just four days after the Tynecastle victory, when Celtic travelled to Ibrox for a rearranged league fixture. Kenny started a Celtic attack in midfield with a delightful flick to Roy Aitken, who in turn passed to Craig. Joe then swivelled and sent an unstoppable twenty yard shot high into the net. This proved to be the winning goal. It was an tremendous psychological boost as it was Celtic's first victory over Rangers since January 1974. Before the game Kenny had eruditely stated to newspaper reporters: *'Celtic v Rangers games are all right. So long as you win.'* Unfortunately the victory was not without cost for Celtic, as their last Lisbon Lion, Bobby Lennox, broke his leg in a controversial challenge by Rangers' captain John Greig.

Kenny had now grown into his role as Celtic captain, and the signings of Stanton and Craig had taken some of the burden from him. Craig's power in attack meant that Celtic were no longer reliant on Kenny scoring, and Stanton composed the defence, which was no longer leaking soft goals.

Captains tend to fall into two camps, those who motivate loudly and those who lead by example. Kenny's leadership style was the latter. Stanton remembers a captain who was respected by his team mates but also someone who also had a lighter side: *'As a captain if he had anything to say he would say it and players would take it from him as he was a great player. He wouldn't talk down to anyone and everyone was treated the same. He led by example and he had a presence. Sometimes in training he would take a turn in goals but even at training he still had that great desire to win. The pressure was there every game to win at Celtic and he was a great competitor. He loved silly jokes in the dressing room, daft ones like you would get in Christmas crackers. People may not be aware of it, but he had a funny side to him.'*

Celtic continued their fine league form throughout the winter months. On 8th January Kenny enjoyed a mixed day at Tannadice, on his 300th appearance for Celtic. In the first half he lashed home one of his trademark thunderbolt shots, but in the second half he missed a penalty. After United equalised Celtic had a real fight on their hands, before a late John Doyle goal gave them a 2-1 win. Three days later Celtic faced Rangers in a rearranged

New Year fixture at Parkhead. Jock Stein was so keen to get the game played that he brought in an army of volunteers to cover the pitch with hay to prevent frost from damaging the turf. The effort was worthwhile because the pitch was declared playable, and Celtic won 1-0 on a bitterly cold night, moving above their great rivals in the league table. On 18th February Kenny became a father for the second time when Marina gave birth to their son Paul. Twenty four hours after the happy event Kenny celebrated by scoring twice against Ayr United at Somerset Park, in a 4-2 victory.

....

English media cast an envious eye at Jock Stein.

There are only two men with the qualifications to take over as England manager from Don Revie. His immensely experienced and respected club rival, Jock Stein of Celtic, and my original preference after Alf Ramsey's departure in 1974, Ron Greenwood. Stein, I believe, would give England the continuity Revie has been unable to establish.

Daily Mail, 16th February 1977

....

Celtic were on course for the league title and the Scottish Cup when a transfer which rocked Scottish football was announced. Former Rangers star, Alfie Conn, had been looking for a move from Spurs. Jock Stein stepped in to sign him in a sensational move. Stein had thought long and hard about going after Alfie, and had even taken the unusual step of consulting Kenny and Danny McGrain to ascertain their opinions. Both men were totally behind their manager so Stein pressed ahead with the move. Rangers were rumoured to have been considering making a move of their own, but Stein got in first and persuaded Alfie that his future lay at Parkhead.

Conn looked like a different player after linking up at Celtic Park. The long hair, sideburns and facial hair were all gone and he sported a new, clean shaven look. Years afterwards, when Alfie was asked to name his most difficult opponent, he amusingly replied: *'The barber when I first joined Celtic!'* Conn made his debut on 5th March at Pittodrie. He appeared as a substitute as Celtic lost their first league game since their previous visit to Aberdeen in October. Alfie made his home debut the following Wednesday against Partick Thistle, and was given a rapturous reception by the Celtic faithful when he scored in a 2-1 win.

....

Welsh rugby legend Phil Bennett tells how he could have become a Celt.

When I was 14 I had been playing a lot of football as well as rugby. I was asked to go to West Ham for a month's trial, and I played for Swansea youngsters when I was 15. Then a chap arrive and asked me if I wanted to go for a month's trial with Glasgow Celtic. I didn't go and soon after I had to decide whether I was going to play rugby or football. I haven't been unhappy with my choice.

Daily Record 19th March 1977

....

During a seven day period in March Celtic played two games which all but clinched the league title for them. At Ibrox they faced Rangers, who had to win to keep their slender title hopes alive. In the first half Celtic played some terrific football, and led through a Roy Aitken goal. Two opportunist goals from Derek Parlane then gave the Ibrox men the lead, before another Aitken effort deservedly levelled the score at 2-2. One week later, Dundee United came to Parkhead. They were in second place, just three points behind Celtic. The game was described as a tale of two penalties. In the first half United were awarded a penalty. In an unusual move their goalkeeper, Hamish McAlpine, stepped forward to take the kick. Roy Baines was making his debut in the Celtic goal in place of the injured Peter Latchford, and became an instant hero when he saved McAlpine's effort. In the second half Celtic were awarded a penalty. However McAlpine was unable to redeem himself, and Ronnie Glavin scored to help Celtic to a 2-0 win.

Pat Stanton had settled quickly into Celtic's system and was a most influential player in Jock Stein's new set up. He explains how impressed he was with Kenny as a team mate: *'At Celtic, when I had the ball at halfway, Kenny would be further forward. He would be marked by a defender and had a midfield player in front of him, so he would move away towards the midfielder and the defender would then leave him. What he was doing was finding space and I could then shove a ball forward for him to turn in that space and run at goal. The guy who should have been marking him would then realise too late what was happening. Kenny would take balls in tight areas and he had the ability to turn a bad pass into a good pass. He had great peripheral vision. He had a boyish look but he was very strong and very quick over a short distance. He saw things early which gave him a yard. To the great players the first couple of yards is all in the head.'*

On Sunday 27th March Kenny was guest of honour at the Celtic Supporters' Association rally in Glasgow's Kelvin Hall. One thousand people crammed in to see him given his award by the official supporters' body. The award was not given as a *'player of the year'* gesture, but was an annual presentation to an individual for long standing service to Celtic. Kenny was in his tenth year as a Celt, and this honour was richly deserved.

In the programme, John McPhail rated Kenny as one of the greatest Celtic players ever, with the following testimonial: *'My own association with Celtic dates back to 1941, when I realised my life's ambition and signed for the club for £20. Previous to that I was in attendance at matches since 1932 , so perhaps I can talk with a certain amount of authority on the great Celtic players of the last forty years. My own particular favourites have been Jimmy McGrory, Malcolm MacDonald, Jimmy Delaney, Willie Buchan, Charlie Tully and Jimmy Johnstone. I would rate Kenny at least equal if not in fact superior to all but Jimmy Johnstone. And even wee Jimmy could never kick a ball with the power and accuracy of Kenny.'*

On 13th April Celtic travelled to Fir Park knowing that one point would give then their first Premier League title, and also give Kenny his first honour as captain. It turned into a disastrous night, and Motherwell beat Celtic 3-0, which was something of a freak result. Celtic's unfortunate left back, Andy Lynch, had the misfortune to score two late own goals. As team captain, Kenny typically sprung to Lynch's defence when interviewed by the Evening Times in the days after the game: *'Someone actually asked me after that game what I said to Andy. They must be kidding. I said absolutely nothing to him - we all knew how he was feeling. We do not point the finger at individuals. If we win we all take the credit, if we lose we all take the blame.'* Three days later Celtic were due to play at Easter Road. The *'battle of the greens'* was one of the most anticipated games of the Scottish football calendar. Sadly, Hibs' chairman Tom Hart used the fixture for his own agenda. Hart had long been a critic of televised football and stated that cameras would be banned from filming Celtic's visit to the capital. He was roundly condemned for waiting until the thirty third game of the season to take this stance, and his action was seen as vindictive, especially when he also banned the amateur Celtic Film Club from filming the game.

The truth may have been that Hart had an ulterior motive, as he was likely to have been envious of Glasgow's big two winning the title on his Easter Road pitch. Celtic had won there in 1973, Rangers in 1975, and Celtic were about to do so again. Hart may also have been annoyed at the prospect of Pat Stanton returning to win the league title on his old stomping ground. Hart and the

Hibs' management had been heavily criticised for allowing fans' favourite Stanton to leave Hibs, especially given his subsequent tremendous form for Celtic. In the end Hart action's cost Hibs some much needed finance. The attendance was 22,000 when in excess of 30,000 had been expected, with many Celtic fans staying away due to the spiteful actions of Hibs' chairman.

If Lynch was the villain against Motherwell, then he redeemed himself against Hibs. After 38 minutes he cleared an Arthur Duncan shot off the line, with Peter Latchford well beaten. In the second half Celtic grabbed the only goal of the game, when Joe Craig scored from an Alfie Conn cross. After the final whistle there were great scenes of jubilation as Celtic took the acclaim of their supporters, with a delighted Kenny hoisted high on the shoulders of his team mates, holding a Celtic scarf aloft. After the match Kenny mentioned his relief to the Evening Times at captaining Celtic to a trophy at last: *'Sometimes at the back of my mind I did wonder if it was becoming a bit of a jinx. But that's silly talk. You do need luck to win anything but I believe that to a great extent a team makes its own luck especially in the long slog for the championship.'*

For Pat Stanton there was delight at winning his first league medal at the age of 31, but his big day had been slightly soured: *'Winning the league at Easter Road was great but when we were celebrating no one from Hibs management came through to say well done after all the years of service I had given them. I hadn't been in the away dressing room since the days of the first team versus the reserves in the early 1960's and it was a strange experience to be back there.'*

On 27th April Kenny had the great privilege of being named as Scotland captain for the International match against Sweden at Hampden. The honour of captaining his country meant a great deal to him, and he described his commitment to Scotland through the media: *'I've just been made captain and I've had forty caps so I can't be that bad. I always regard it as a great honour to wear the Scotland jersey and like everyone else in the team I try my heart out.'*

Whilst the Scotland team were preparing for the game Scottish sportswriters announced that Danny McGrain had been voted Scotland's Player of the Year for 1977. This was a richly deserved award for McGrain, who had enjoyed an exceptional season for both Celtic and Scotland. Sadly for Kenny, this would be his last opportunity to win this prestigious award. It's difficult to believe that a player of his talent was never recognised as Scotland's player of the year. However he is in good company, as Jimmy Johnstone did not win it either.

Dalglish and McGrain were Scotland regulars, and they were joined by team mates Ronnie Glavin and Joe Craig, who were making their international debuts. Kenny scored in a 3-1 win, but the game is best remembered for Joe Craig's goal. Craig had just replaced Kenny Burns in 76 minutes, when he scored with his first touch, a header, from a Sandy Jardine cross. This gave rise to the popular quiz question - Which player scored for Scotland before he'd kicked a ball? Joe still remembers meeting Jock Stein after the game: *'I was walking along the Hampden corridor, feeling quite proud, and Mr Stein passed me and said, 'You did okay Craig but you should have had a hat trick,' and walked on by.'*

The Scottish Cup final was to be contested between Celtic and Rangers on 7th May. For the first time the final had a sponsor, Scottish and Newcastle Brewers. The game was to be shown live on television by the BBC and STV, the first televised final since 1955. Celtic received a blow in the days leading up to the final, when high scoring midfielder Ronnie Glavin failed a fitness test, having being injured during the Scotland v Sweden friendly. This prompted Jock Stein to change his tactics and deploy a three man central defence, with Pat Stanton sweeping up behind Roddy MacDonald and Johannes Edvaldsson. Kenny was deployed in a midfield role, and Paul Wilson was recalled to replace John Doyle in attack. Stein knew that Edvaldsson and Wilson both had an endearing habit of performing well against Rangers, and this was the thinking behind their selection.

The Celtic team were in their dressing room preparing for the game when a telegram arrived for Pat Stanton. A bemused Jock Stein passed it to Stanton to open. It was a goodwill message from his former Hibernian team mates, telling him to *'complete the set'*. This was a reference to the fact that Pat only needed a Scottish Cup winners medal to go with the League and League Cup honours he had already won. This was a wonderful gesture from his former Easter Road colleagues, and it gave Stanton a great lift before the big match.

In the run up to the final, Jock Stein held a penalty contest to determine who would take any penalties awarded during the match. With regular penalty taker Ronnie Glavin injured, Andy Lynch was a surprise winner, and it was decided that he would take any penalties on the day. As fate would have it, Celtic were awarded a penalty in the 20th minute, when Derek Johnstone handled the ball on his own goal line. There was consternation amongst the Celtic fans when Lynch stepped up to take it, not least from his own father, who had no idea that Andy had assumed penalty duties. Kenny, realising that Lynch may have been nervous, actually offered to take it, but Andy was determined and sent a fine low shot past Stuart Kennedy in the Rangers' goal.

In the second half Celtic missed the best two chances of the game. Joe Craig was straight through on goal and missed by inches, before a thrilling run by Danny McGrain set up Paul Wilson, who miskicked from six yards out. The ball then broke to Craig who saw his shot scrambled off the line by Colin Jackson. With seconds left Celtic were given a huge scare when young Rangers striker Chris Robertson sent a powerful header crashing against the crossbar.

Celtic held on and Andy Lynch was the unlikely hero of the hour. Lynch recalls how Celtic won the tactical battle: *'Playing Johannes Edvaldsson worked like a dream. He was told to mark Derek Johnstone, Roddy MacDonald was to look after Derek Parlane, with Pat Stanton left to sweep up at the back. It couldn't have been better arranged because Derek Johnstone didn't get a kick, or more importantly a header at the ball. Jock Wallace was a great big guy, a lovely human being; I had been coached by him at Tynecastle when I was with Hearts. But frankly, his tactics against us were naive. All they were doing was punting high balls into the penalty area whenever they had possession and that was right up our street. We perhaps concentrated a bit more on defence but Joe Craig up front was more dangerous than the two Rangers strikers put together and Kenny Dalglish was always a threat to them'*

Kenny was now a Scottish Cup winning captain and proudly led his team up the Hampden staircase to receive the trophy. It appears that the excitement of winning the trophy may have affected him. Firstly, after being presented with the trophy, he walked away with it and the other Celtic players had to shout after him to bring it back so that they could each raise the cup in the traditional fashion. Then he managed to lose his medal in the after match celebrations, as he later explained to Archie McPherson, in his book, ' *The Blue and the Green'*: *'We were running around the park when we came to the spot where three or four kids were sitting in wheelchairs. I stopped and asked one of them if they wanted to see my medal. The medal was in a presentation box and I lifted it out but just then someone jolted my arm and it spun forward. Immediately I started scrambling on the ground trying to find it. Some of the lads and Neilly Mochan helped me. There is a kind of wooden skirting board separating the pitch from the track at Hampden and because I thought it had fallen down there Peter Latchford and I started to rip it up. But we couldn't find it and I don't mind admitting that I was nearly in tears about it all. The police told me it was better to go back in the dressing room and let them find it. I had every confidence in them.'*

Kenny's medal was returned by Chief Inspector Michael Hamill, brother of Strathclyde's Chief Constable, Patrick Hamill. He came into the dressing room to say that it had been found down the inside of a fan's umbrella. Kenny was understandably delighted to be reunited with his medal and stated his intention to present it to his baby boy, Paul. As if he hadn't already been absent minded enough, as Kenny and Jock Stein left Hampden with the trophy they inadvertently tried to board the Rangers bus. Jock Wallace was photographed playfully waving his fists at them, as the Celtic pair headed back to their own bus in embarrassment.

One disappointing aspect of the final was the attendance. Over 70,000 tickets had been sold, but rain on an unseasonably cold day, and live television coverage of the match reduced the attendance to 54,000, the lowest post war crowd for a Scottish Cup final. As cup final sponsors, Scottish and Newcastle were enraged to discover that rival brewers, Tennents, had purchased advertising boards behind each goal. This gave them greater television exposure during the final, and at a fraction of the price paid by the official sponsors.

There is a fascinating story as to what happened to Kenny's 1977 cup final jersey in later years, as Sean Pinkman explains: *Leslie's Bar in Edinburgh in the 1980's was where I first got to know Sandy Jardine. At that time Sandy and Alex McDonald were the management team at Hearts, and that bar on a Saturday night was a great after match venue. Sandy, Terry Christie, (manager of Meadowbank Thistle), and players from various teams would all meet there after their respective games and myself and some fellow Celtic supporters would meet up with them when we returned from watching Celtic to discuss the days games. As the friendship grew we were invited to Sandy's 40th birthday held at his house in December 1988. Shortly after this Sandy's daughter, Nicola, got married to my friend's son. Next up was my friends 50th birthday and we decided there was no finer place to celebrate it than the Barge Inn, Leitrim Village in County Leitrim, where we had all been a few times before. However Sandy could not join us on this occasion but asked me to*

THE LAST HURRAH - 1976/1977

keep an eye on Nicola as this was her first trip to Ireland. Needless to say a great time was had by all, especially Nicola. A few weeks after our return, Nicola's husband came to my house with a gift from Sandy. It was Kenny Dalglish's 1977 Cup Final jersey, which he had swapped with Sandy, and this was a gift from Sandy for looking after Nicola. I was totally stunned and when I next met up with him he said, 'You would appreciate this more than me having it lying up in the attic.' I have always believed that items like Kenny's Jersey should be shared with people who would appreciate seeing it, so on our next trip to Ireland, which was to Aranmore Island, County Donegal, I took the jersey over and give it to Pally McHugh to display it in his pub for all to see. To bring the story to its conclusion, sadly Sandy and Pally have passed away, but the jersey is now kept in Pally's son John's house in Donegal.

Celtic had provisionally arranged a game against Inter Milan to celebrate the 10th anniversary of their European Cup win in Lisbon. It was scheduled for 24th May. However, the match had to be cancelled as Celtic had agreed to provide players for the Glasgow Football Association's game against the English League. Inter offered to play in early June but McGrain and Dalglish were in the Scotland squad, and the other Celtic players had already arranged holidays. The Glasgow FA had arranged the match as part of the city's celebrations to commemorate Queen Elizabeth's silver jubilee. Kenny had the privilege of being captain, and presented the Glasgow players to her before the match. The Glasgow strip was described a *'hideous concoction'* of the colours of the five city clubs. The English side contained a few big names such as Dave Watson, Trevor Francis, Mike Channon and Denis Tueart. The Glasgow team ran out winners by 2-1, with Kenny scoring the winning goal. A trophy was to be presented to the winning captain, although the Queen had departed by then for another engagement. Scotland manager Willie Ormond was in charge of the Glasgow side, and had just announced that he was leaving to take the manager's position at Hearts. Kenny insisted that he should go up and collect the trophy, which was a tremendous gesture that Ormond very much appreciated.

As part of the European Cup anniversary celebrations, a function was held for the Lisbon Lions in the Odeon cinema on Glasgow's Victoria Road. As Celtic captain Kenny was asked to say a few words, and he was cheered to the rafters when he stated that he wanted to lead Celtic to victory in the following season's European Cup. This was to be a prophetic statement from Kenny, but sadly he was not to be wearing green and white when he finally did lift the European Cup at Wembley in May 1978.

Dalglish and McGrain had a busy end to the season when they represented Scotland in the Home Internationals, and also went on a three game tour of South America. Scotland won the Home International championship for the second successive year, with the victory over England at Wembley being the highlight. The Scots were now under the stewardship of flamboyant manager Ally MacLeod, and Kenny scored the winning goal in a 2-1 win, a scrappy effort in which he just managed to edge the ball over the line.

In South America Scotland were scheduled to play against Chile, Argentina and Brazil. The fixture against Chile was most controversial as the country was under the rule of military dictatorship. General Pinochet had led a military coup in 1973, and the National stadium in Santiago, where the game was to be played, was said to have been used to hold political prisoners. The SFA agreed to play there against public and political opinion, and Archie McPherson recalls an incident from Scotland's short time in Santiago: *'In Chile there was a military dictatorship and one day we were sitting around the pool and this very well dressed, suave gentleman with impeccable English came to us. He started to wander around talking to the players and we quickly realised that he was a mouthpiece for the Pinochet regime. The players were quite reserved but when he approached Kenny he was given a mouthful of Glaswegian and told where to go.'*

In Santiago, Ally MacLeod reunited Kenny with his old Celtic pal Lou Macari. The partnership flourished, with Lou scoring twice and Kenny once. Scotland turned in an impressive performance, and won 4-2. MacLeod was impressed by the pair, who knew each other so well from their Celtic days. In Buenos Aires Scotland gained a respectable draw with Argentina. They then they travelled to Rio where they lost 2-0 to Brazil in the Maracana.

One year later, Ally considered reuniting the pair for Scotland's ill fated game against Iran in the 1978 World Cup in Argentina. He lamented afterwards that it had been a huge mistake not to do so, and things might have been very different for Scotland and for Ally had he played them.

The last game in Rio was played on 23rd June, and for Kenny a long, arduous season was over. Celtic fans spent their summer looking forward to their team's challenge in the European Cup. They were not to know that storm clouds were gathering over Celtic Park.

CHAPTER TWELVE
ABDICATION - SUMMER 1977

In 1976 Kevin Keegan informed the Liverpool management of his intention to leave Anfield in the summer of 1977, in order to play his football abroad. He would eventually sign for Hamburg SV. Keegan was the most high profile player in England, famed for his appearances on television adverts for Brut aftershave and his participation in the BBC's highly popular TV show, *'Superstars'*. This was a huge blow for Liverpool, but they had advance warning of his departure and were in the market for a replacement. Their attention was fixed on Celtic Park as Billy McNeill was to discover: *'I travelled to Rome to see Liverpool beat Borussia Munchengladbach in the European Cup final in May 1977. I was in amongst the Liverpool fans and they were saying 'We're going to sign Kenny Dalglish from Celtic.' I said you've got no chance and I believed it.'*

Kenny's contract with Celtic had expired shortly before the Scottish Cup final. He agreed to sign a new contract, to avoid causing any controversy before the big match. However, he made it clear to Jock Stein before signing that he intended to leave in the summer and take his talents south of the border. Stein was keen for his captain to stay, and on Kenny's return from Scotland's South American trip he tried to persuade him that his future was at Celtic, but Kenny remained determined.

Celtic were due to leave for a six game tour of Singapore and Australia in early July. It was a prestigious tournament, also involving Red Star Belgrade and Arsenal. The organisers were obviously keen to have the teams field their best players, and Stein tried to persuade Kenny to go. Dalglish was said to be exhausted from a season in which he had played almost seventy games, and Stein eventually agreed that Kenny could stay home to consider his future, with young Celt Jim Casey replacing him in the squad which travelled abroad. Jock must have earnestly hoped Kenny would have had a change of heart by the time Celtic returned in early August. As the Celtic players arrived at Parkhead for the bus to Glasgow airport, they were aware of one noticeable absentee. Joe Craig recalls: *'When the bus left without Kenny we knew then that he was off. He had confided in some of us that he was going to Liverpool but we thought he wasn't serious.'*

Kenny trained at Parkhead whilst the team were abroad, as Celtic youth player of the time, Brian Coyne remembers: *'When the team went to Australia for pre-season 1977, Kenny didn't go. He stayed and everyone was concerned that he would be leaving. He trained with the boys who were left behind, mainly reserve and 'S' form signings. At that time everyone had practically resigned themselves to the fact that he was going to go. It was still a shock when it actually happened especially for those of us who were Celtic fans as well as Celtic players. We all wanted him to stay and were excited to be training with him. He had a presence and he was great with the boys.'*

Stein had tried to play down Dalglish's absence by saying that the player needed rest. This didn't stop the media pouncing on the story, especially when news filtered north that Liverpool had identified Dalglish as a ready made replacement for Keegan. Celtic returned home from their travels as tournament winners, and Stein made it his priority to persuade his captain to stay, but all to no avail. Kenny remained adamant that he wanted to depart.

The lure of English football and the finances associated with it were obvious to any Scottish player. Kenny must also have considered that Celtic's last three European campaigns saw them lose to Olympiakos, Sachsenring Zwickau and Wisla Krakow, hardly the cream of European football. He wanted to play at the highest level in Europe. This was a frustration for Stein as he felt his new Celtic team, with Stanton, Craig and Conn now bedded in, could make an impression in the European Cup. The signing of Alfie Conn had been controversial. It was later considered that Stein may have signed Conn as a potential replacement for Dalglish, in view of his possible departure. The newspapers were full of speculation regarding a potential Dalglish transfer, but Celtic fans hoped that things would die down again as they had done previously, in August 1975.

On 7th August Jock Stein told the Sunday Mail that he was still hopeful of resolving the matter in Celtic's favour: *'Kenny Dalglish will play against Dunfermline on Tuesday and against Dundee United on Saturday, unless something happens during the week. The player has made no demand for a move and there is no dispute over finance. I've had talks with him this week and there is no question of him being disciplined for not going on tour. We're hoping that everything will be resolved before the opening league match but we'll see.'*

Unknown to the public and the media, Stein had finally relented and agreed to let Kenny go. On 9th August Celtic visited East End Park for a low key friendly against Dunfermline. The first thing the Celtic fans would have noticed was that Danny McGrain led the team on to the field as captain. It was after this match that Kenny realised a transfer was finally on, when journalists informed him that Liverpool manager Bob Paisley, and chairman John Smith, were in attendance in the stand. Archie McPherson retains a memory from that night in Dunfermline: *'The day before he left there is a photo of Kenny running on to the park at East End Park, Dunfermline, which shows Jock looking down on him like a father who is saying farewell to his son.'*

Celtic and Liverpool met after the match to discuss a transfer fee. There was a certain naiveté on the part of Celtic chairman Desmond White, as he did not seem to have a figure in mind, and was ready to accept Liverpool's first offer of £300,000. Jock Stein intervened and eventually pushed Liverpool towards a fee of £440,000, perhaps in a forlorn hope that Liverpool might withdraw from the deal should the player prove too expensive. Liverpool agreed to the higher fee. The Celtic delegation were unaware that Liverpool had fully intended to offer £500,000 if required, which was the entire fee received from Hamburg SV for Kevin Keegan. Liverpool were fortunate to have the Keegan transfer money to spend, as no other British club was thought to have been able to afford Dalglish at that time.

After a 4-1 win at Dunfermline Kenny went back to Pat Harkins' pub with Peter Latchford. Stein later called the Dalglish home, asking for Kenny to come to Parkhead urgently, and Marina relayed the message to her husband. On his arrival at the ground Jock made one last appeal for Kenny to stay, but without success. Stein then drove Dalglish to Moffat to meet the Liverpool representatives and complete the formalities. There was a certain irony in Kenny's choice of team. In 1967 he had joined up at Parkhead shortly after Celtic had been crowned as European champions. Ten years later and he was joining Liverpool, who were the reigning European champions. It's said that Jock's last words to Kenny were, *'Good luck, you wee bugger.'*

CHAPTER THIRTEEN
AFTER THE KING HAS GONE

On the morning of 10th August 1977, Celtic fans awoke to the devastating news that Kenny Dalglish had departed for Liverpool. Many older fans stayed away from work, such was their distress on hearing the news. Younger fans, enjoying their summer holidays from school, were also sad and disillusioned. Many a Dalglish poster was torn down from a bedroom wall in frustration.

Kenny sent the Celtic supporters a farewell message through the Daily Record: *'I wish I had been able to make a farewell in front of the fans at Celtic Park They have been tremendous to me ever since I joined the club. I've left now but I won't forget the supporters and I won't forget the club or the people there.'*

....

Let's be honest. Kenny Dalglish will be a loss to Scottish football but who can blame him for grabbing his golden chance. We wish him well. Still it makes you think. If you have a youngster, why try to make him a Professor or Prime Minister...when he could be worth £440,000 for kicking a ball.
Daily Record editorial, 11th August 1977

....

Celtic chairman Desmond White revealed some startling details of Kenny's transfer to the press: *'It is true that Kenny Dalglish did not ask away and that had we wanted he would still be with us today.*

It was, however, a very complex issue. We were loath to let him go but it got to the stage where he was practically incapable of giving his best to Celtic...and only best is good enough. He did not ask for a transfer but all the indications were he was unhappy. We know that inside his soul he was unhappy at Celtic. It was not unreasonable to sound out sources with a view to his transfer for the sake of the good of the player as well as the club.'

Dismayed Celtic fans read his statement with incredulity, and their reaction was an angry one. They swamped the newspapers and the Celtic View, expressing outrage at the betrayal which allowed Dalglish to go. White's statement begs the question which has tormented Celtic fans for many years: Could Celtic have done more to keep Kenny at the club at that time? The answer is, undoubtedly, yes.

In 1977 there was no freedom of contract for footballers, and the Bosman ruling was a long way off. Provided a player was offered at least the same terms as the previous season he was not entitled to a transfer, so Celtic were in a very strong bargaining position. Dalglish could only be sold if Celtic agreed to sell him. This would have left them with a very disgruntled player, but the truth is he would not have been the first footballer to have been refused a transfer.

At the time of the transfer Celtic were a limited company, which meant that they had a very small shareholder base compared to clubs who were public companies. Celtic shares were not available on the open market, and could only be bought and sold with the agreement of the Celtic board. With £440,000 to be banked, there would have been a considerable dividend paid out at the yearly AGM, so financially Celtic directors and shareholders stood to benefit from Kenny's transfer.

Sir Robert Kelly ensured that none of Celtic's Lisbon Lions were sold at their peak, and he would never have countenanced a transfer to the detriment of the club. Dalglish's transfer was yet another example of Celtic chairman Desmond White being too ready to sell for big transfer fees. White's mantra was that Celtic did not wish to keep unsettled players. The fans were left to wonder why did Celtic's best players always seem to be unsettled?

The Celtic directors could have offered Kenny a financial inducement to remain at the club. They could also have negotiated a lucrative testimonial for him, as he had ten years service at Parkhead. There was no more popular player in the country, and a testimonial would have been highly beneficial to Kenny financially. A game against top English opposition would have guaranteed a full house, and the proceeds from such a match would have been considerable. Although Celtic maintained a stable wage structure, they could have considered making Dalglish a special case with a salary considerably higher than the other players. The supporters recognised he was exceptional on the field of play, and in their view he was regarded as irreplaceable. The Celtic board should also have appreciated this.

Celtic were also missing a vital link in the bargaining process. Sean Fallon, at the time on the periphery at Celtic Park, was adamant that he could have persuaded Kenny to stay. Before he passed away in 2013, Sean admitted to his biographer, Stephen Sullivan: '*Kenny came to our house in King's Park the day he left and he was breaking his heart. I still don't believe deep down he wanted to go. It proved the right decision in the end but I definitely think that, if things had have been handled in the right way, we could have kept Kenny for a year or two more. But by that stage the board weren't even trying to keep him. They couldn't wait to sell and Jock wasn't able to stop them.*'

Davie McParland had replaced Sean as Stein's assistant manager, but he and Kenny did not develop the close bond that Kenny and Sean had enjoyed. When Kenny returned to Parkhead to collect his boots McParland was the last person he saw before leaving. There was to be no emotional goodbyes with Fallon, Bob Rooney or Jimmy Steel, the much valued back room team who had been instrumental in Kenny's development as a player.

Celtic were left to pick up the pieces without their talisman player. Hugh MacDonald recalls: *'Most supporters were pragmatic enough at that time to know he was going to go. There was a huge sadness about that. The Lisbon Lions had only left later in their careers and now Hay and Dalglish had left in the peak of their careers, which was hard to take. The size of the fee was annoying because Liverpool made a profit out of selling Keegan to Hamburg. What Liverpool were getting was the finished article. They weren't signing a blossoming talent.'*

Archie McPherson observed changing times within the club: *'It was a watershed when Kenny left. A major star was leaving Celtic. Jock had moved on the Lisbon Lions, but at his own pace. When Kenny left, Jock lost a bit of power. I wasn't aware of Kenny leaving in advance but I don't think he was getting enough money wise.'*

Ex-captain Billy McNeill had also tried his best to influence his old team mate to stay, as he later told the Evening Times: *'Kenny lived round the corner from me and I tried to persuade him not to go to Liverpool. I said your heart is here in Glasgow. But he was single minded. He had everything planned out the way he wanted it to be. He was 26 and he had served Celtic well and had achieved a great deal with them.'*

Down south, a delighted Bob Paisley exclaimed: *'I feel I have got the best player in Britain. We owed this to our supporters.'* Bill Shankly, former Liverpool boss and great friend of Jock Stein, was typically blunt, and struck a chord with Celtic fans. *'I understand that like Kevin Keegan, Dalglish wants to get on, but I would have moved heaven and earth to keep him. I would rather have quit and got out of the game altogether than sold a player of his brilliance.'*

Celtic had a huge £440,000 cheque to bank, but were to discover that they could not readily spend it. The Celts could not hope to replace Kenny, at any price, but they never seriously attempted to do so. They could have purchased one of the up and coming young talents such as Paul Sturrock of Dundee United, Mark McGhee of Morton or Frank McGarvey of St Mirren. However perhaps it was felt they were not ready for such a huge challenge in the early stages of their careers.

In this modern age of football Celtic routinely sign players from England, Eastern Europe, Scandinavia and have even ventured into the Far East and South American markets. However, in 1977 they could only realistically sign players from the Scottish Leagues. One player who could perhaps have helped Celtic's cause was Motherwell's talented striker, Willie Pettigrew. Following Dalglish's departure, Celtic stood to lose an average of thirty goals per season. Pettigrew was a high scoring attacker and was in dispute with Motherwell. He was a natural goal scorer and could have been purchased for around the £150,000 mark. Although he was not regarded as being in the same class as Dalglish, his signing would have been a clear message from the Celtic board that the club meant business, and would have been something of a boost for the supporters.

In August 1977 it was reported that, *'the King has gone'*, when Elvis Presley died. Celtic fans shared the sentiment, but with reference to Kenny's departure.

When researching this book it was surprising to speak to a number of people who recalled Elvis dying first and then Kenny leaving Celtic. It was actually the other way around, with Kenny leaving on 10th August, and Elvis Presley sadly passing away on 16th August. For Celtic supporters of the period, Kenny's departure to Liverpool would be regarded as their *'JFK moment'*, when they would always recall when and where they were when they heard the devastating news of his departure.

Joe Sullivan recalls: '*As a 17-year-old I used to walk from Barmulloch down to Royston Road in Provanmill to get the bus to work and would usually bump into some mates there doing the same. I can still remember being at the same bus stop on two different mornings in August of 1977, less than a week apart. Two items of news were broken to me by the very same mate, John Ward, as he walked towards the bus stop reading the morning paper. One of them was that Elvis Presley had died – and that meant absolutely nothing to me! It meant little to any of the group of mates at that bus stop who travelled to the games together. The other, just a few days earlier, was broken with the words: 'Kenny's away!'... that was different. To be honest, the only reason I remember where I was when Elvis Presley died was because it was on the exact same spot where I found out that Kenny was away...the real King...King Kenny. A bunch of us huddled around the paper looking at a picture of a resigned looking Jock Stein watching Kenny take to the pitch for the last time in a friendly at Dunfermline. Somebody uttered the words: 'Just when we had a good team for Europe!' I also remember going to the pictures with my girlfriend around that period. I can't remember what the movie was, but recall being excited when I saw that the one of the support features was a short film called 'King Kenny'. I was bit miffed when it actually turned out to be about some motorcycle guy, who I had never heard of, called Kenny Roberts.'*

One thing that Kenny left Celtic fans with was memories, and there were plenty of them. Mike Maher recalls some his favourite Kenny moments: *'I once asked Billy McNeill who was the best player he had played with or managed. His answer was Kenny and I would not disagree. I saw the Lisbon Lions in their prime and Kenny was better than any of them. Right from the start you could see how good he was. My father once said Kenny never had any potential – he was always just brilliant. Henrik Larsson would shade him due to his greater athleticism but in fairness that was not needed so much in Kenny's era. Along with Danny McGrain, Bobby Murdoch and Jimmy Johnstone, Henrik and Kenny are the real genuine 'world class' players Celtic have had in my time. You have got to be careful when reminiscing, but I cannot recall Kenny ever having a bad game. Some weeks he was not as good as others but that only emphasised his high standards. The best performance I saw from him was against Dundee in November 1974. Indeed that was by far the best individual performance I ever saw from any Celtic player. Wee Jinky did perform out of his skin against Red Star Belgrade in 1968 but that was mostly just the second half. It was a different style too. Jinky was like a 'hyper kid' who had just had a shot of sugar. He ran about daft! Kenny at Dens was more imperious. We won 6-0 with Kenny scoring three and making the others. For the last goal he must have ran from his own half beating player after player before flicking it past the keeper.'*

Some fans such as George Murray, found it hard to come to terms with his departure: *'When Kenny was sold I was very bitter about the way it happened and for years could not bear to watch him with any joy - it was too painful. The press tried to make out that his success at Anfield was all down to Liverpool's superior training methods. I wrote to the Herald, which was one of the papers peddling this myth. I pointed out that the Liverpool doctor on the day of the transfer had said that Kenny was the fittest player he had ever examined! What really stuck in my craw was that Liverpool had just sold Keegan for £500,000 and that Desmond White had accepted less for Kenny - a palpably better player and the captain of our club. Clearly he was playing with better players at Liverpool, and that helped, but Kenny was the hub of all that was good during their glory years, and we never saw anything similar until Henrik Larsson arrived - apart of course from Danny McGrain, who before his injury was the best player I ever saw in the green and white.'*

Lawrence Murphy has good reason to recall each anniversary of Kenny's departure from Celtic Park, with some religious significance: *'I will never, ever, forget that Kenny left us on 10th August. With the anniversary and feast day of St Lawrence being on the same date, I have an annual reminder of how I felt that day in 1977 - devastated. That day something inside me died.'*

James Doyle reflects: *'For me, what makes a great player is the ability to do the simple things. Kenny was capable of scoring the most wonderful individual goals but he was also one of the most unselfish players I have ever seen. If there was a simple pass on he would always make it, and he set up a lot of goals for other Celtic players at times when he could easily have gone for glory himself. He was the perfect team player, always available to take the ball in difficult situations, and he was brave too. The amount of punishment he took from defenders was terrific but he never reacted. His combination play with Danny McGrain was exceptional. Watching the two of them together there were times I thought they were telepathic, so good was their understanding of each other's game.'*

Tom Joyce recalls that some Liverpool fans were not aware of the quality of player they had just signed: *'In August 1977 I took my wife and family on holiday to Rhyl, in North Wales. My oldest son, Kevin, was sent to the newsagents each day to get a Daily Record so I could keep up to date with events back home. One day he came back empty handed and said that the Glasgow papers hadn't arrived. The next day he came back with a paper, and also the previous days' edition which had arrived a day late. I took the kids down to a working men's club to read the papers and get some refreshments. When I looked at the paper I was stunned to see Kenny explaining why he left Celtic. I then looked at the previous days' copy to see that he had been sold to Liverpool. At the next table there were a few men who heard our Glasgow accents. They wanted to know my opinion of Kenny, and they said that no matter how good he was he would never be able to replace Kevin Keegan in the hearts of the Liverpool fans. They were completely unaware of Kenny's talents. I told them that he was the best player in the UK and that they would not be disappointed.'*

The pain felt following Kenny's departure was to take a long time to heal. David Potter recalls: *'I was once travelling between Moscow and Leningrad. On the train I met a Moscovite whose English was as rudimentary as my Russian. I was anxious to avoid being mistaken for a German or an Englishman so I said that 'Shotlandia' was my country. The man from Moscow beamed, 'Ah, Shotlandia! Boorns, Monstr, Dalglish!'.' Boorns was a poet, Monstr lives in Loch Ness and the mention of the third, even after many years, still caused me distress.'*

Charles Murray recalls a frustrating advert shown at the *'pictures'*: *'Dalglish's departure was a big disappointment, leaving a scar which never truly healed, remaining raw even to this day. In the late 1980's there was a cinema advert for a particular brand of Scots whisky, (the name I can't recall), which began: 'Scotland through the ages has lost all its national treasures – The Stone of Destiny...Bonnie Prince Charlie... North Sea oil...Kenny Dalglish...' God, I hated that advert. It was clearly an attempt at humour and I squirmed in the cinema seat every time, because Scotland didn't lose Kenny Dalglish, Celtic did. He was easily the best player in British football at that time. Celtic fans were given a constant reminder of their loss in the following years, as Liverpool blazed a trail across Europe, winning everything in sight. Dalglish was their brightest talent, instantly recognisable by his huge, distinctive smile, which he flashed after every goal scored. He was a loss alright - a huge loss. Kenny should have had 'made at Celtic' tattooed on him. In his time at Parkhead he inherited the passing skills of Murdoch, the guile of Auld and the competitive spirit of Wallace, which as we all know now was a potent mixture indeed.'*

Perhaps the greatest written testament to Kenny's time at Celtic can be found in David Bennie's hugely enjoyable and entertaining book, *'Not Playing For Celtic'* - *'For seven years Celtic supporters had the pleasure of seeing a footballing genius play week in and week out, and in every game Dalglish never gave anything less than the clichéd 110 per cent. We had been privileged to see Dalglish scoring great goals, laying on memorable assists and covering every blade of grass with the grace of an Arab thoroughbred, and the heart of a Clydesdale workhorse. In his time at Parkhead Dalglish regularly transformed ordinary sporting contests into extraordinary exhibitions of performance art.'*

For those who remember Kenny Dalglish, in Celtic's famous hoops, the memories will always remain. The grace of movement, the balance when running with the ball, the sudden swerving turns which flummoxed the opposition. But perhaps the most abiding memory of all will be that beaming smile, hair drenched with sweat, arms aloft in triumph, running to his adoring supporters after scoring a wonder goal.

The last quote should come from the great man himself: *'Celtic gave me a hell of a lot and I believe I gave them everything I had to give in return. That is the way it should be in football.'*

KENNY IN THE GREEN

You grew up in Ibrox shadow
with their heroes on your wall
that all changed
in the glorious May
when Sean Fallon called.

You were now Kenny of Celtic
the best there's ever been
the jungle roared loudest
when you wore the green.

Your arrival was announced
in a place you knew so well
memories of support
faded
with a gallus
pause
to tie your lace
then choose your place
to stroke the penalty home.

From Boghead to Brockville
you turned patchy parks to gold
breezing by defenders
turning
twisting
tight
close control unrivalled

the Celts roared
at the sight
of you
rounding numerous goalies
dancing with ease
a red cheeked wonder
who we didn't want to leave.

We never tired of you
taking the acclaim
with a smile
as wide as the Clyde
all boyish looks,
foppish hair
arms up
palms wide
reaching for the stars
when the stars
should have been reaching for you.

You were as close to perfect
as we have ever seen
Kenneth Mathieson Dalglish
or King Kenny in the Green.

By kind permission of Kevin Graham

KENNY DALGLISH CELTIC STATISTICS

Appearances:

Year	League	League Cup	Scottish Cup	Europe	Total
1968/69	-	1	-	-	1
1969/70	2	2	-	-	4
1970/71	3	-	1	1	5
1971/72	31	8	4	7	50
1972/73	32	11	6	4	53
1973/74	33	10	6	7	56
1974/75	33	8	5	2	48
1975/76	35	10	1	5	51
1976/77	35	10	7	2	54
Total	204	60	30	28	322

Goals:

Year	League	League Cup	Scottish Cup	Europe	Total
1968/69	-	-	-	-	-
1969/70	-	-	-	-	-
1970/71	-	-	-	-	-
1971/72	17	5	1	-	23
1972/73	23	10	5	3	41
1973/74	18	3	1	2	24
1974/75	16	3	2	-	21
1975/76	24	4	1	3	32
1976/77	14	10	1	1	26
Total	112	35	11	9	167

KENNY DALGLISH LEAGUE GOALS

13 - Ayr United

12 - Motherwell

9 - Heart of Midlothian

9 - Saint Johnstone

8 - Hibernian

8 - Dundee United

7 - Dundee

6 - Aberdeen

6 - Kilmarnock

6 - Clyde

5 - Partick Thistle

5 - Falkirk

4 - Rangers

4 - Dumbarton

4 - Arbroath

3 - East Fife

2 - Dunfermline Athletic

1 - Airdrieonians

HAT TRICKS

16 Oct 1971   Celtic 3 - 1 Dundee

14 Dec 1974   Dundee 0 - 6 Celtic

6 Oct 1976   Celtic 5 - 0 Albion Rovers

First competitive appearance:
25 Sep 1969 v Hamilton Academical (League Cup)

First League appearance:
4 Oct 1969 v Raith Rovers

First Scottish Cup appearance:
7 Apr 1971 v Airdrieonians

First Euro appearance:
30 Sep 1070 v Kokkola

First competitive goal:
14 Aug 71 v Rangers (League Cup)

First League goal:
4 Sep 71 v Clyde

First Scottish Cup goal:
26 Feb 72 v Dundee

First Euro goal:
27 Sep 72 v Rosenberg

50th League goal:
29 Dec 73 v Dunfermline Athletic

100th League goal:
23 Oct 77 v Aberdeen

50th competitive goal:
3 Feb 73 v East Fife (Scottish Cup)

100th competitive goal:
14 Dec 74 v Dundee (League)

150th competitive goal:
6 Oct 76 v Albion Rovers (League Cup)

Scotland appearances: 47

First cap:
10 Nov 71 v Belgium

Last cap:
23 Jun 77 v Brazil

Note: Kenny became Celtic's most capped player when he played against Argentina in 1977.

Scotland goals: 16

First goal:
15 Nov 1972 v Denmark

Last goal:
15 Jun 1977 v Chile

Note: Kenny scored 16 goals for Scotland during his Celtic career compared to 14 in his time at Liverpool.

Statistics kindly compiled by Roddy Stewart.

ACKNOWLEDGEMENTS

My formative years as a Celtic fan coincided with Kenny Dalglish's breakthrough into the Celtic team as a first team regular. I stood beside my Dad and his friends on the old Parkhead terraces and we drooled over Kenny's displays in the hoops. He seemed far more intelligent than the other players on the pitch, with his fantastic array of feints, dummies, sublime touches and general reading of the game.

One morning in August 1977 I recall my Dad waking me early and calling me into the living room. He always bought a Daily Record each morning before leaving for work at Govan shipbuilders. He showed me the paper, and as my eyes strained to focus, I learned that Kenny had signed for Liverpool. I never asked my dad why he woke me early that morning, during the school holidays, but I reckon he just wanted someone to share the bad news with. Like all Celtic fans, we were devastated.

The main reason behind writing this book is that Kenny's time at Celtic has never been fully chronicled. Many books about his career provide a greater focus on the Liverpool years, which is no surprise given his outstandingly successful period at Anfield. However, he was ten years a Celt and this hugely important period of his career deserves much greater recognition.

This book could not have been written without the assistance of some extremely supportive people. My grateful thanks go to journalist Hugh MacDonald, for providing a terrific foreword to the book. Thanks also to Roddy Stewart, (perhaps Kenny's biggest fan), for the detailed statistics of Kenny's Celtic career and to Jason Henderson for helpful suggestions.

I was fortunate enough to speak with some fascinating people who all readily shared their memories of Kenny - Archie McPherson, Rodger

Baillie, Kathleen Murdoch, Hugh Keevins, Pat Stanton, John Fallon, Joe Craig, Andy Lynch, Jim Delahunt, Chic Young and Brian Coyne. Grateful thanks to them all.

My appreciation is extended to the Cumbernauld United trio of Eric Drever, George Watson and John Kirk for providing detailed information and their personal memories of Kenny from his time at the junior club. To this day they still cherish the memory of Kenny in the Cumbernauld colours.

Thanks also goes to those who answered my call for memories of Kenny through Celtic websites and fanzines. They have provided a wealth of affectionate recollections of Kenny's time at Celtic, and it was amazing to hear from those who kept Kenny scrapbooks, souvenirs and memorabilia from his time at Parkhead. My thanks to Terence Dolan (who kept a photo of Kenny in his hall and would allow no one to enter the house unless they bowed before it!), Chris McPhail, George Curran, George Sheridan, George Murray, Mark Reeves, Rodney Larkins, Linda Paterson, Mike Maher, John Monteath, Tony Griffin, Frank Balloch, Charles Murray, John Burns, Mike McCafferty, Norman Emerson, Jeanette McCulloch, Tom Stewart (Dublin), Robert Harvey, Joe Sullivan, Sean Pinkman, Catherine Oates, David Potter, Neil Logan, Lawrence Murphy, Brian McKenzie, Jim McGinley, Tom Joyce, Matt McGlone, and James Doyle.

Special thanks to Brian Gallagher and Brendan Sweeney for their invaluable assistance with my research.

Thanks also to Stephen Cameron for the book design and to Paul Brennan and David Faulds at CQN books.

And finally, special thanks to Susanne (editor in chief!) for her painstaking hard work in making this book read so well. And to Mikey, for his suggestions, and for reminding me what it is like to see Celtic through the eyes of a child.

BIBLIOGRAPHY

Daily Record

Evening Times

Glasgow Herald

The Celtic View

The Celtic Wiki

The Quality Street Gang (Paul Dykes)

Sean Fallon - Celtic's Iron Man (Stephen Sullivan)

Celtic Greats (Hugh Keevins)

And You'll Never Walk Alone (Gerry McNee)

The Blue and the Green (Archie McPherson)

Dalglish (Stephen Kelly)

Kenny Dalglish soccer annual (1979 and 1980)

King Kenny (Ken Gallacher)

Ten Days That Shook Celtic (David Potter)

Playing for Celtic (Rodger Baillie)

Not Playing For Celtic (David Bennie)

Dalglish - My Autobiography (Kenny Dalglish)

There's Only One Dixie Deans (Dixie Deans)

*Photographs by kind permission of Daily Record, Glasgow
Herald, Celtic View, David Connelly and Chris Hanratty.*